Change of Heart

Change of Heart

A Wesleyan Spirituality

By JAMES A. HOPWOOD

WIPF & STOCK · Eugene, Oregon

CHANGE OF HEART
A Wesleyan Spirituality

Wipf & Stock
An Imprint of Wipf and Stock Publishers
199 W. 8th Ave., Suite 3
Eugene, OR 97401

www.wipfandstock.com

PAPERBACK ISBN: 979-8-3852-0551-6
HARDCOVER ISBN: 979-8-3852-0552-3
EBOOK ISBN: 979-8-3852-0553-0

VERSION NUMBER 12/01/23

This book is for those churches I served in the Kansas City and Lawrence areas of Kansas, especially for members of Edgerton United Methodist Church. All were a receptive audience for many of the ideas explored here.

Contents

Acknowledgements

I gratefully acknowledge the Spirit-guided influence of many mentors mentioned in this book, as well as many others who are not named. I also must thank two people who have kept me on the right way in the writing of this book. My wife, Linda, encouraged me throughout and made helpful comments on early drafts. My friend and former seminary professor Hal Knight also read an early draft and made valuable comments, including several that kept me from some serious howlers. Any remaining blunders are purely my own, of course.

Introduction

"**O**h happy day, another book about John Wesley!"
I live in a house with many books by and about John Wesley, so I understand the ironic lament. Do we really need *another one* right now?

As the United Methodist Church—the largest Wesleyan body in the world—splinters, I think the time is right for a brief popular introduction to Wesley and the Methodist movement that he founded with his brother Charles. I offer this book not only for its brevity and succinctness but also for the personal witness it offers for how I became and why I remain United Methodist. This book breaks no new ground and is not intended to. It's intended simply to introduce readers to Wesleyan spirituality.

I am not a Wesley scholar, but as a retired United Methodist pastor I have a longtime interest in all things Wesleyan, and I have read deeply in Wesley studies. I am especially indebted to Henry H. "Hal" Knight III, with whom I studied at St. Paul School of Theology thirty years ago. He also was a seminary mentor to my wife, Linda, and remains a good friend to our family.

Outside of a few broad strokes, this is not a history of Methodism in America, or even in Britain. You may wonder, then, why I offer so much detail about Wesley's life. That's because his theology arises from his personal experience as well as from his study, prayer, and inspiration of the Holy Spirit. His theology follows his spiritual development and matures as he matures spiritually. Though he does not often acknowledge being wrong, even he admits that some of his early formulations were inadequate or faulty. Sometimes, as he "argues with himself," you can almost see his mind at work.

Wesley is not a systematic or academic theologian, so he's sometimes not taken seriously by academics who love systematics. In the Anglican tradition, he focuses on practical theology, plain speaking for normal people. He has little patience with speculative theology. For example, he offers no insight into the inner life of the Trinity, and he doesn't try to explain how sin is transmitted from one generation to another, or how communion "works," or precisely *how* Jesus' death saves us. These are interesting topics, and plenty of other theologians explore these things. Wesley does not see them as "necessary for salvation," so I don't either.

I call Wesleyan spirituality a way of life that follows the Jesus Way. To appreciate it, you have to understand that all ways do not lead to the same destination. "The Way" of a Christian cult by that name is different from "the Way" of the Tao in Confucian and Taoist thought, and both are different from the vacuous "This is the way" of the Star Wars TV series *The Mandalorian*.

The Jesus Way, in sharp contrast to those other ways, has a specific content that is presented to us in the Bible, brought to life by inspiration of the Holy Spirit, and interpreted by us through tradition, reason, and experience. The early Christian movement is several times called "the Way" (Acts 9:2; 19:9; 19:23; 24:14; and 24:22). Images of walking in the right way or the right path occur throughout both testaments of the Bible. (I'm thinking especially of Ps 1 and Isa 35:8, which speaks of "the Holy Way" or "the Way of Holiness.") Similarly, the *Didache*, a first-century manual of Christian life, notes that there are two very different ways of existence, one that leads to life and one that leads to death.

The Jesus Way—the Wesleyan way, the Methodist way—is a way of orienting your life to God, the meaning of life, and your purpose as a human being. As the United Methodist baptism ritual states, it is "the way that leads to life." It is my intention and prayer that this book may help you on that Way.

A NOTE ABOUT NOTES

Throughout this book, I allow Wesley to speak for himself with little editing. That means you'll sometimes encounter archaic language, including male references to God and humanity in general. Outside of quotations, I use inclusive language and avoid portraying God as male.

Each of the six chapters is followed by comments on related hymns by Charles Wesley, and by Six Good Questions for reflection or discussion, plus a suggestion for reading one of Six Great Sermons by John Wesley. At the end, I offer a list of Wesley resources that I have found especially helpful. Some are more challenging reading than others.

I have included many footnotes in the hope that they will lead inquiring readers deeper into Wesleyan theology. Notes quoting John Wesley follow this format:

Sermon 5, "Justification by Faith," II.1, Works 5:56
That is:

• Number and title of sermon, journal entry, or publication.

• Paragraph of subsection of the document.

• Source name, volume number, and page number in the fourteen-volume Thomas Jackson edition of Wesley's *Works*.

I use Jackson rather than the newer Bicentennial Edition because it is more accessible to most people. However, excellent internet sources may make access to either collection unnecessary. The Christian Classics Ethereal Library, for example, offers a PDF file that can be downloaded and easily searched.

1

A Way of Life

My father was raised Baptist, and my mother was raised Roman Catholic. They solved the family religion problem by not going to church at all. I received no formal religious training until the third or fourth grade, when I started attending a fundamentalist church with some cousins who lived nearby. That church is where I first heard about the people called Methodist. I heard that Methodists were godless heathens who were going to hell.

I left that church early in college. I asked the pastor for guidance in a matter that was important to me, involving the application of faith to daily life. Instead of guidance I got shallow religious platitudes and a lecture on obedience to authority. I vowed to never again set foot in that or any other fundamentalist church. I was churchless for several years. It never occurred to me that those godless Methodists might offer something worthwhile.

There was a large Methodist church on my college campus, but I never entered it, though I came close. For most of one semester, my girlfriend and I spent several nights a week in the nearby Wesley Student Center. We camped out in a small anteroom dedicated to John Wesley. The walls of the room were lined with glass-fronted shelves filled with books by and about Wesley. I had never heard of him, and I never cracked a single book with his name on the spine. Sometimes I wonder how my life might have changed if I'd read from Wesley then, knowing nothing else about him.

There's another sad aspect to this little story. We went to the Wesley Student Center to study because it was quiet. I'm a retired United Methodist pastor who strongly supports campus ministry, so it pains me deeply to say that although we felt welcome at this campus ministry center, I don't recall anybody ever actually *telling* us that we were welcome, or why. The place was always open, but there didn't seem to be much going on, and I don't remember many friendly faces. It was easy for us to slip in and out, apparently unnoticed. So we did.

At her suggestion, we did attend a Unitarian church for a short time. It sponsored a great coffeehouse, and we hoped that the atmosphere of that place reflected what the church was like. Not so much. It had a beautiful Gothic-style sanctuary, a powerful organ, and a good choir. But the word "God" came up only occasionally, and then only in some of the old hymns, where it couldn't easily be excised. I don't think I heard the name "Jesus" even once. The whole exercise seemed pointless to me. The congregation received us politely but not especially warmly. We were college students; no use getting to know us because we'll be gone soon anyway. And so we were.

Several years later, out of college and in my first job as a newspaper copy editor, I met Linda. Her grandfather had been a Methodist pastor in Ireland and then in Kansas and Florida. I figured if I was going to get serious about marrying her, I'd better learn what this Methodist stuff was all about. To my pleasant surprise, I found it to be the most congenial form of Christianity I could imagine. I was hooked—and I remain so today.

When I say that I found Methodism congenial, I don't mean easygoing or loosey-goosey or any of the other sad clichés that some people use to smear Methodism. Rather, I mean that I found Methodism friendly and hospitable and, most of all, firmly aligned with the teachings of Jesus. How so? That's part of what we'll be looking at in this book, which I offer as a brief introduction to Methodism and Wesleyan spirituality.

Methodism is a religion of the heart. You might not guess that after attending some of the lifeless exercises that pass for worship

in some Methodist churches. Still, it's true. Methodist Christianity—or, Wesleyan Christianity, if you like—is a heart religion. It's
about warming your heart and changing your heart. By changing
your heart, I don't mean merely tinkering with it or repairing it. I
mean *replacing* it. As God told the prophet Ezekiel (36.26): "I will
give you a new heart and put a new spirit in you. I will remove your
stony heart and replace it with a living one." Yes, major surgery is
involved. We are in the heart transplant business.

I once knew a man named Dennis who had received a heart
transplant. He was eventually killed by the drugs that he took to
keep his body from rejecting the heart. But he marveled that those
drugs and that heart gave him eleven years with his loved ones that
he would not have had otherwise. The transplant also gave him a
new perspective on living. He wanted to cherish every moment
because he had come so close to having no more moments.

No scalpels are involved, but the spiritual heart transplant
that we are talking about *will* change you too. It will bring you
to new understandings of what it means to be human, what it
means to be spiritual, and what it means to be alive. We call it the
Wesleyan Way. This way is named after the Wesley brothers, who
were priests in the Church of England in the mid-1700s. It was a
time of great religious ferment in England as well as its colonies in
America. While Jonathan Edwards and George Whitefield were
igniting the religious revival known as the First Great Awakening
in America, John Wesley and his brother Charles were fanning the
flames of the Methodist Revival in Britain.

The way the Wesley brothers pioneered is, first and foremost,
a way of following Jesus. Jesus is the Way, the truth and the life
(John 14.6), so to the extent that the Wesleyan Way is true to the
Jesus Way, it is a way of truth and a way of life. Jesus is the author
of life, and his way is the way of salvation, so the Wesleyan Way is a
way of life that leads to salvation (Acts 3.15, Acts 16.17).

Notice two things immediately. First, notice that I say the
Wesleyan Way is "a" way of following "the" way of Jesus and "a"
way that leads to salvation. Wesleyans do not claim that ours is
"the" one and only legitimate way of following Jesus. We do not

claim that we have a monopoly on God's truth. Other churches *do* make such claims, and they are sadly misguided. We know that there is a wideness in God's mercy and a greatness in God's grace that far exceeds our human capacity for loving others. Others can restrict God's love to themselves—but, happily, Scripture assures us that God is greater than our hearts, and God's grace is larger than our human prejudices (1 John 3.20).

Notice secondly that I refer to the Wesleyan Way as a way of life. I call it a way of life rather than a "religion" because the words "religion" and "religious" have fallen into serious disrepute. "Religion" now implies an oppressive means of controlling people, and "religious" has come to mean self-involved, closed-minded, and bigoted. Of course, that's the exact opposite of what the words *should* mean. The English word "religion" comes from a Latin word having to do with reconnecting things and binding them together. True religion is almost exclusively about healing relationships. It's about reconnecting God and people. Truly religious people are those who are rightly related to God and to others.

The Wesleyan Way is a way of following Jesus. It's a way of being in relationship with God and other human beings, as well as with the rest of God's creation. It's a way of living that is true to the teachings of Jesus and therefore a way that leads to salvation and happiness.

Let's look briefly at that word "salvation." A lot of people talk about "getting saved" as if it were a one-time decision, and that's all there is to it. Say yes to Jesus once and you're saved. You've got eternal fire insurance. It's like a "Get out of hell free" card. Your ticket to heaven has been punched; you are good to go. When that train that's bound for glory is ready to roll, you have a reserved seat on it.

Sorry, but that is a very limited, distorted, inadequate, and ultimately destructive way of thinking about salvation. Throughout the gospels, many people come to Jesus for both physical and spiritual healing, and Jesus heals their afflictions. What he does, in fact, is *save* them. The New Testament uses the Greek word *sozo*, meaning "to heal" and "to make whole" and also "to save." Versions of that word mean health, wholeness, and salvation. To be

4

saved is to be made healthy, to be made whole, to be set right. The Wesleyan Way of salvation is about being set right with God and others and made healthy and whole in the process. It's more than a one-time event. It's the journey of a lifetime.

The goal of the journey is neither avoiding hell nor getting into heaven, though a lot of people think that. The goal of the journey is becoming the persons God created us to be—and that means persons who are just like Jesus. That's why the journey can take a lifetime. We are broken people, each and every one of us. We are so broken that the deep healing we need may involve a long process. But God is willing to invest all of God's love in us in the hope that we will respond by loving God and neighbor in return and thus fulfilling our purpose as human beings.

The goal of this process goes by two names. Both are profoundly misunderstood in our time. Those two words are *holiness* and *happiness*. The words are closely related, though not quite synonymous. Holiness is living in the image of Christ in loving communion with God and others. Holiness leads to happiness, so that a life of holiness is a life of happiness, and a life of happiness is a life of holiness. The rest of the world doesn't think so, but in the Wesleyan Way of thinking, happiness is more than a good feeling, and holiness has little to do with following a long list of stifling rules. You were intended to be just like Jesus, John Wesley says. You were created to be holy. You were created to be happy.

Let me introduce you to several key terms that I think define Wesleyan spirituality and the Wesleyan Way of salvation. Here they are, with a few verbs sprinkled in to show how they fit together.

> **God's love** is revealed by **grace.**
> It sparks **repentance** and inspires **faith.**
> It ignites **rebirth** and animates **holiness,**
> *creating* **happiness.**

Notice where this starts? It starts with God's love. For Wesley, everything starts with God's love. And where does it end? With happiness, or holiness—two words that describe a way of living in God's love, two words that describe the rule of God in a person's heart, a foretaste of the very kingdom of God whose coming Jesus announced.[1] So God's love encompasses everything.

We'll return to this summary in more detail as we go along. For now, simply understand that Wesleyan spirituality is a journey toward happiness in this life and the next. It's a way defined as much by quality as it is by quantity, a life of such abundance that it begins right here and now and overflows into eternity.

This is why you were made, John Wesley says. "You were *born* for nothing else. You *live* for nothing else. Your life is continued to you upon earth for no other purpose than this—that you may know, love, and serve God on earth and enjoy him to all eternity."[2] Check out that list of verbs: know, love, serve, and enjoy. When and where? Here and now, but not *only* now. Now and forever.

"Consider!" Wesley continues. "You were not created to please your senses, to gratify your imagination, to gain money or the praise of [others], to seek happiness in any created good, in anything under the sun. . . . On the contrary, you were created for *this*, and for no other purpose, by seeking and finding happiness in God on earth, to secure the glory of God in heaven."[3]

The path to such happiness, the way that leads us there, Wesley calls "true religion." He says it can be shown in two words: "gratitude and benevolence—gratitude to our Creator and supreme Benefactor, and benevolence to our fellow creatures. In other words, it is loving God with all our heart, and our neighbor as ourselves."[4]

Methodists are often criticized for "reducing" the gospel to the love of God and neighbor. Some critics get apoplectic. "Where do you get the idea that the whole Bible can be boiled down to this? Where do you get the idea that loving God and being loved by God is what life is all about?"

Where do we get this idea? You probably know where we get it. We get it from Jesus. He is the one, after all, who was asked

1. Sermon 7, "Way to the Kingdom," I.10–13, Works 5:80–81.
2. Sermon 109, "What Is Man?" 15, Works 7:230.
3. Sermon 109, "What Is Man?" 15, Works 7:230.
4. Sermon 120, "Unity of the Divine Being," 16, Works 7:269.

which was the greatest of God's commandments. How did he answer? He said: "Love the Lord your God with every fiber of your being, with all your heart and all your spirit and all your mind and all your strength, and love your neighbor as yourself" (Matt 22:36–40; Mark 12:28–31; Luke 10:25–28).

God's love will enable and empower you to do that, Wesley says, and thereby live a life of holiness and happiness. Happiness does not necessarily mean a life of ease, without discomfort. Nowhere in Scripture are we guaranteed a journey without hills and valleys, potholes, bumps and curves, detours and dead ends. We *are* guaranteed that because we know that God is with us every step of the way, we can find true joy in the journey and true happiness now and forever.

I invite you now to travel with me to explore the Wesleyan Way of following Jesus, a spirituality that leads to a total change of heart. Some of the path covers familiar territory. Other parts you may find less familiar, perhaps even new and surprising. Let's walk together on this way.

As we begin our journey, remember Wesley's description of it. You were created for *this* and for no other purpose. You were *born* for this and you *live* for nothing else. Your goal in life is to find true happiness by knowing and loving and serving God on earth and enjoying God to all eternity. Doesn't that sound like a wonderful way of life?

MAVERICKS

Early in June of 1742, the Rev. John Wesley is traveling nearly the full length of England, from Newcastle in the north to London in the south. He decides to stop about halfway in between at Epworth, his childhood home, where his father served as vicar (parish pastor) for forty years and where he served in his father's place in Samuel Wesley's last days.

Wesley asks whether he might preach at the parish church, or at least assist with one of its Sunday services. The resident vicar, who lives in the large brick parsonage that Samuel Wesley built with his own money, says he may not.

Soon, a friend passes word that Wesley, denied use of the church *building*, will preach that evening in the church *yard*. A large crowd assembles, and Wesley preaches while standing on his father's gravestone. He returns every night for the next week, continuing to draw crowds, before resuming his journey to London.

Wesley is used to being rebuffed at churches. It has happened many times in the four years since he started preaching salvation by faith alone. It's not that his message is heretical. It is, in fact, the established doctrine of the Church of England. But it's the *way* he preaches it. He fires people up. He preaches "unguarded," one worthy tells him. "It is dangerous. It may lead people into enthusiasm or despair."[5]

Both enthusiasm and despair are great fears in England at the time. After two centuries of bitter struggle and even violent civil war over religion and politics, people at all levels of society are edgy about any emotional appeal that might spark civil unrest. As a result, the church keeps such a low profile that it is barely visible in some places. Meantime, the coal-fired Industrial Revolution burns hot, transforming the economic and social face of the nation. Thousands of rural people flock to the cities seeking jobs and a better life and find mostly poverty and deprivation.

Wesley is mindful of the social cost of the Industrial Revolution, but he has a different sort of revolution in mind—a revolution of the heart. He and his younger brother, Charles, intend "to reform the nation, particularly the church, and to spread scriptural holiness throughout the land."[6]

The church doesn't especially want to be reformed, at least in the way the Wesley brothers want to reform it, so it fights back. Usually the church employs passive-aggressive means of resistance, but many times individual vicars work to turn people against them and even incite riots to drive them away. Through it all, the Methodist movement prospers and grows—from a dozen

5. Journal, Nov. 24, 1739, Works 1:250.
6. "Large Minutes," 3A, Works 8:299.

or so students in a college dormitory to a religious revival that involves thousands and shakes the core of a nation—for the better.
Indeed, the movement prompts such positive social change that
some historians say it helps England avoid the kind of violent social and political revolution that convulses France even as John
Wesley nears his final breath.

Evangelism is the Wesley brothers' main concern. They want
to bring people into a life-changing relationship with God through
Jesus Christ. But mere proclamation of the gospel is never enough
for them. They want to fully live out their mandate to love God
and neighbor, so they are always working to do good for others at
every opportunity.

Their list of such accomplishments includes:

- Many forms of ministry with those held captive by poverty or
  imprisoned for debts because of it.

- Orphanages and free schools, including the Kingswood
  School, founded in 1748 and still running today.

- Housing for older widows.

- Short-term interest-free micro-loans.

- Free medical dispensaries, including a clinic run by John
  Wesley himself.

- Publication of a best-selling medical guide titled *Primitive
  Physick: An Easy and Natural Way of Curing Most Diseases.*

- Publication of the *Christian Library*, cheap, abridged versions
  of fifty Christian classics.

- Publication of cheap editions of hymns by Charles Wesley
  and others.

- Public opposition to slavery and the diversion of crops to
  liquor rather than food.

The Wesleyan Way, or Methodist Way, thus embraces evangelism *and* social action. John Wesley is an integrative thinker.

His approach is both/and rather than either/or.[7] Following the Anglican tradition of *via media*, or "middle way," he tries to steer a faithful straight course between various extremes. Wesley is well-schooled in many Christian traditions, and his thinking incorporates the best from Lutheran pietist to Reformed and Puritan, Anabaptist, Roman Catholic and Eastern Orthodox. Methodists have also been influenced over the years by African American, Native American, Hispanic, and Korean traditions. The result of this rich conglomeration of influences has sometimes been called the "Methodist synthesis." It holds together word and sacrament, law and gospel, faith and works, personal and social holiness, divine initiative and human response, grace and responsibility, piety and sacramentalism.

In his lifetime John Wesley publishes more than two hundred books, magazines, tracts, and broadsides, including a four-volume history of England and a book titled *Birds, Beasts and Insects*. It is estimated that in his fifty-two years of itinerant ministry, he travels more than 225,000 miles, mostly on horseback (and by carriage only when aged). He preaches at least forty thousand times.

Though Charles is not remembered today as a preacher, he also travels many thousands of miles and preaches thousands of times. Charles is most widely remembered, of course, for his hymns. He writes upwards of 9,000 hymns and sacred poems, publishing perhaps half of them in his lifetime—more than 50 volumes of work over fifty-some years. With Isaac Watts, he revolutionizes English hymnody. Where before Anglicans mostly droned psalms during worship, these two give them theologically profound hymns worth singing with gusto.

John is known to catch up on his reading while riding, trusting his horse to stay out of trouble on what are, by all accounts, terrible roads. Charles is known to arrive at some destination, leap off his horse, and immediately ask for pen and paper so he can record the lyrics to a hymn he composed on the way.

The story of the Methodist movement is basically the story of these two brothers and their answer to God's call in their lives.

---

7. Chilcote, *Recapturing*, 11.

John lived from 1703 to 1791, Charles from 1707 to 1788. There are times when it's not possible to sort out their individual contributions because they freely preach each other's sermons and don't always distinguish who wrote what part of what hymn. History shortchanges the role Charles plays because it's usually easier to quote John, who is clearly the figurehead and leader of the Wesleyan branch of the Methodist Revival.

John Wesley is a man of many contradictions held together in creative tension, very much like the theology he weaves throughout his life. You can view him as a man who is by constitution and training pulled in one direction but by the grace and power of the Holy Spirit is propelled in other directions.

He is an Oxford don who feels most at home teaching Greek grammar in the sheltered halls of academia, yet he spends fifty years preaching outdoors and in industrial halls, mostly to people of very little education. He accepts the rigid social structure of his time as the will of God, and yet he empowers people of all social classes as leaders of his revival and fosters one of the most truly democratic social movements of the eighteenth century.

Though he opposes warfare of any kind, he is a Tory and intensely loyal to his king, so he volunteers to raise a regiment should England be invaded by France. He thinks the American colonists are crazy to rebel against the crown, but when they win their freedom—"by a very uncommon train of providences"[8]—he accepts the separation as God's will and is pleasantly surprised to learn that Methodism has leapfrogged the Atlantic without him.

As a priest of the Church of England, he is trained to be an ally of the aristocracy, yet he distrusts people with wealth and prefers the company of poor people. He deeply loves the Church of England, yet he openly opposes its power brokers whenever he thinks they are wrong. After frequent struggles with doubt early on, he grows steadily more self-assured, strong-minded and strong-willed. As a leader he can be rigidly authoritarian, but he's still open to hearing the opinions of others.

8. Wesley, *Sunday Service*, i.

He calls himself a man of one book, and he reads the Bible from cover to cover at least once every year. He is so thoroughly familiar with Scripture that he can scarcely speak a sentence without unconsciously quoting Scripture. Yet he reads and appreciates many books, across many disciplines, and he encourages his followers—especially his preachers—to do the same.

His restless mind leads him to scientific investigations such as experimenting with electricity, as Benjamin Franklin is doing at about the same time. He even invents an "electrifying apparatus" to deliver electrical impulses to sore muscles—a primitive TENS unit. His faith occasionally leans toward superstition. He's known to practice the "lucky dip" method of Bible reading, in which you trust God to lead you to a Scripture that will speak to your present situation. (At least it gets you to open a Bible.) When Wesley can't reach a decision using the Bible or reason, he may cast lots, figuring that God will control the outcome. (That has some scriptural precedent, such as deciding who should replace Judas as the twelfth disciple. Yet it seems to rely more on chance than on God—unless you trust that God micromanages every move you make.)

Charles mostly defers to his older brother's leadership, but John could not be who he is without Charles' steady influence. They are temperamentally quite different. John is a compulsive perfectionist and somewhat cool emotionally. Charles is an outgoing and emotional romantic. John is energetic and appears tireless. For fifty years he rises at 4 a.m. and preaches at 5 nearly every day. Born prematurely, Charles is troubled by poor health all his life, especially after a terrible winter in the wilds of Georgia with little food or heat.

Both are short, even for their day (5 foot 3, tops), and slightly built. Still, they are considered handsome young men who need to be watched around the ladies. Charles marries at age forty to a woman half his age whom he meets at a revival meeting in Ireland. They have a good marriage and produce eight children, only three of whom survive childhood (sadly, a common story in their time). John cultivates many deep spiritual friendships with women, but proves inept when it comes to romance. He suffers several awkward courtships and finally marries at age 46. It's a disaster almost from the start.

Both remain priests in the Church of England till the day they die. But over the years Charles grows more and more suspicious that John is moving away from the church and soon will be Anglican in name only. John thinks the practical need to save souls overrides all human conventions—including those of the church— and he is much more willing than Charles to deviate from church tradition. That disagreement eventually leads them to drift apart.

They were born into similar disagreement. Their parents, Samuel and Susanna, both come from families headed by pastors of nonconformist, or dissenting, churches—that is, churches that are tolerated but officially discriminated against because they are not Church of England (and probably have Puritan leanings). But both Samuel and Susanna renounce the churches of their youth and join the Church of England. As converts of all kinds tend to be, they are zealous in denouncing what they were before their conversion, and they are known for spirited verbal attacks on nonconformists.

That attitude doesn't sit well in rural and backward Epworth. One man responds to Samuel's attitude about dissenters by having Samuel jailed for a debt. There also is suspicion that locals are responsible for two fires in the rectory. The first causes relatively minor damage to the timber-frame, thatch-roof house. The second burns it to the ground and contributes to John Wesley's legend.

After the parents struggle to get everyone out of the burning house in the middle of the night, a quick head count reveals that five-year-old "Jacky" is missing. One neighbor stands on the shoulders of another and pulls the child from a second-story window just as the roof collapses above him. Years later, when a sick Wesley prematurely writes his own epitaph, he styles himself as "a brand plucked out of the burning." It is, of course, a biblical reference—to either Zech 3:2 or Amos 4:11, in either case referring to one preserved for the sake of mission.

The Wesley family loses all their possessions in the fire and must live with friends and other family members until a new rectory can be built. Samuel pays for it himself, with £400 he doesn't have, and the family is "house poor" thereafter. Not that they were much better off before. Samuel is never paid much, he has to feed a big family, and he has no knack for managing money. John and Charles grow up knowing poverty firsthand.

In a span of nineteen years, Susanna Wesley gives birth to nineteen children, including two sets of twins. Only ten of the nineteen survive childhood—three boys and seven girls. Susanna schools all of them at home, and she is an inventive and skillful teacher. She also is famous—or notorious, if you will—for her strictness and her reliance on corporal punishment. She believes in literally "beating the devil" out of children.

The new Epworth rectory (it still stands and is open for tours) has been called the "cradle of Methodism." Susanna takes great care with the religious education of all her children and devotes one hour every week to one-on-one spiritual conversation with each child. Even after he goes away to school, John asks her to set aside the hour after supper on Thursday nights to remember him in prayer. (Charles' day was Saturday.)

Despite their poverty, John and Charles both get excellent educations, mostly because of scholarships they earn and maintain through scholastic honors. In 1714, when he's ten, John goes off to the prestigious Charterhouse boarding school in London. A scholarship from there sends him to Christ Church College at Oxford in 1720. Charles attends the even more prestigious Westminster boarding school in London, where Latin is the primary language of discourse. He then goes to Christ Church, Oxford, also on scholarship.

Where some children today might take the bus or train or even a plane home on occasion to visit far-away family, John and Charles have no such luxury. Over objections from their father (who can't afford to help them anyway), they walk the whole way—all 150 miles between London and Epworth and back. It's just the start of their long journey together.

THE METHODIST FAMILY

The Methodist family today is large and far-flung. One umbrella group, the World Methodist Council, says it is "made up of 80 Methodist, Wesleyan and related Uniting and United Churches representing over 80 million members in 138 countries."[9] Included in this count are 2.6 million members of the Church of the Nazarene, 1.5 million in the Free Methodist Church, and about half a million in the Wesleyan Church. Not included are many millions in the Salvation Army and various Pentecostal churches, all of which can trace their origins to the Holiness movement within the Methodist Church.

The largest Methodist denomination is the United Methodist Church, which has more than twelve million members worldwide, about half of those in the United States. That number is slipping as some churches disaffiliate and move to the new Global Methodist Church.

The "United" part of the name comes from the 1968 merger of the Methodist Church with the Evangelical United Brethren. The EUB arose from two originally German-speaking churches with strong ties to Methodism: the Church of the United Brethren in Christ, founded by Philip Otterbein and Martin Boehm, and the Evangelical Association, founded by Jacob Albright.

Three primarily Black denominations were formed when racism forced Black believers out of predominantly white churches in America: the African Methodist Episcopal Church (AME), African Methodist Episcopal Church Zion (AMEZ), and Christian Methodist Episcopal Church (CME). Another Black church, the Union American Methodist Episcopal Church (UAME), struggles to carry on.

More than twenty other denominations today also identify as Methodist. England, where the Methodist Revival started, can count maybe 170,000 Methodists. Talk of Methodist/Anglican reunion surfaces periodically. So does talk of Methodist/Episcopal reunion in America. It doesn't go much beyond talk, as you might expect.

9. "About Us."

HYMNS OF PRAISE AND LONGING

Methodists have always learned much of their theology directly through the hymns of Charles Wesley. They are among the most memorable and beloved hymns sung in churches of any denomination. We'll conclude each chapter of this book with selections from one or more hymns that reflect themes related to that chapter.

We begin with two praise hymns. The first is "O for a Thousand Tongues to Sing," which might be considered the Methodist anthem. Charles wrote it in 1739 for the first anniversary of his Pentecost "conversion" experience on May 21, 1738. This hymn has appeared in nearly all Methodist hymnals since 1740. Since 1870 it has traditionally been the hymnal's opening hymn. The original version had eighteen verses. Most hymnals contain about a third of those.[10]

O For a Thousand Tongues to Sing

1. O for a thousand tongues to sing my great Redeemer's praise,
the glories of my God and King, the triumphs of his grace!
2. My gracious Master and my God, assist me to proclaim,
to spread through all the earth abroad the honors of your name.
3. Jesus! the name that charms our fears, that bids our sorrows cease,
'tis music in the sinner's ears, 'tis life and health and peace.
4. He breaks the power of cancelled sin, he sets the prisoner free;
his blood can make the foulest clean; his blood availed for me.
5. He speaks, and listening to his voice, new life the dead receive.
The mournful, broken hearts rejoice, the humble poor believe.

What we consider verse 1 is actually verse 7 in the original. It's too bad that the six verses that precede it are rarely sung today. In them, Charles tells the personal story of his May 21 experience.

---

10. "O For A Thousand Tongues To Sing."

O For a Thousand Tongues, original opening

1. Glory to God, and praise and love be ever, ever given,
by saints below and saints above, the church in earth and heaven.
2. On this glad day the glorious Sun of Righteousness arose;
on my benighted soul he shone and filled it with repose.
3. Sudden expired the legal strife, 'twas then I ceased to grieve;
my second, real, living life I then began to live.
4. Then with my heart I first believed, believed with faith divine,
power with the Holy Ghost received to call the Savior mine.
5. I felt my Lord's atoning blood close to my soul applied;
me, me he loved, the Son of God; for me, for me he died!
6, I found and owned his promise true, ascertained of my part,
my pardon passed in heaven I knew when written on my heart.

Similar themes arise in this 1742 hymn, "O For a Heart to Praise My God." It's a song of praise that's also a plea for renewal—and, of course, an anthem to heart religion.

O For a Heart to Praise My God

1. O for a heart to praise my God, a heart from sin set free;
a heart that always feels thy blood so freely shed for me:
2. A heart resigned, submissive, meek, my great Redeemer's throne,
where only Christ is heard to speak, where Jesus reigns alone:
3. O for a lowly, contrite heart, believing, true, and clean,
which neither life nor death can part from him that dwells within:
4. A heart in every thought renewed, and full of love divine;
perfect and right and pure and good—a copy, Lord, of thine.
8. Thy nature, gracious Lord, impart; come quickly from above.
Write thy new name upon my heart, thy new best name of Love.

SIX GOOD QUESTIONS . . . TO CONSIDER OR DISCUSS

1. Do you follow a "way" in your life?

2. Wesley says God created you to be happy and holy. Are you either one?

3. You were made to "know, love, and serve God on earth and enjoy God to all eternity." How are you doing so far?

4. Wesley is described as "a man of many contradictions held together in creative tension." Could that also be a description of you or others you know?

5. Do you consider the "lucky dip" or casting lots to be superstitious or faithful?

6. Are you also "a brand plucked out of the burning" for a special mission?

Six Great Sermons, #1

"The Way to the Kingdom," Sermon 7, from 1746: True religion is a heart right toward God and neighbor.

2

Who Are You?

W ho *are* you?
    One day some 385 years ago, a French philosopher came
to a conclusion that rocked his world and has seriously warped the
way most of us think about ourselves and everything else.

His name was René Descartes. He was trying to get to the
root of a philosophical problem, to determine once and for all
how to find certainty in an uncertain world. Assuming that doubt
is the opposite of certainty (well, you have to start *somewhere*),
Descartes tried to eliminate everything he could possibly doubt.
Ultimately, he found only one thing that he could not doubt. He
could not doubt that he existed.

So in 1637 Descartes famously concluded, "I think, therefore
I am." In so concluding, he moved the philosophical foundation of
the Western world from trust in God to trust in self. He made humanity the measure of all things. More precisely, he made personal
opinion the measure of all things. It can be argued that in many
ways the world has gone downhill ever since.

Why did Descartes eliminate God as the center of things?
Because he could have doubts about God. He could doubt the
existence of God. He could doubt the *goodness* of God. So, for Descartes, God could no longer be the rule by which all things were
measured. More precisely, Jesus could no longer be the so-called

"measure of a man," and becoming *like* Jesus could no longer be the goal of human life.

In short, not only did Descartes dethrone God. He also de-based humanity.

PRACTICAL THEOLOGY

In these chapters, we are talking about "Change of heart—a Wes-leyan spirituality." We are learning how to live out the theology formulated primarily by John Wesley, who was a leader of the eighteenth-century Methodist Revival in Britain and founder of the worldwide Wesleyan movement.

Wesley was not one to engage in abstruse speculation about the inner workings of the deity. He believed in practical theology—"practical divinity,"[1] he called it, "plain truth for plain people."[2] But he knew well the importance of careful thinking about the nature of God. What you think about God shapes how you view the world, how you view yourself and how you behave with oth-ers. What you believe about God is key to your understanding of everything.

Whether we know it or not, we all draw our identity from God. Scripture says humans were made in the image of God. So the concepts of divine and human are linked. Your identity is linked to God's identity. To properly understand who you are as a human being, you need to properly understand who God is. Some Christians emphasize that God is *transcendent*—that is, "wholly other" than we are, way outside our normal experience. Others stress that God is *immanent*—that is, knowable and present to us in a personal way. In the Wesleyan tradition, we strike for a bal-ance. We find that God is both majestic and personable, somewhat scary yet lovable—and always loving.

It makes a huge difference what kind of God you worship. If you believe that God is a loving parent who wants only what is

---

1. Preface to "Collection of Hymns."
2. Preface to Sermons, 5, Works 5:2.

best for you, you will behave very differently than if you believe that God is a hateful monster who is lurking around every corner waiting for you to mess up so that he can pounce on you and beat you up. An awful lot of people believe in that monster God, and they behave accordingly. An awful lot of those people consider themselves Christian. But hear this plainly. That is not the God revealed by Jesus Christ. The Lord God we worship is no monster. Our God is a loving God, because the loving God is the only one there is. All others are pale imitations and idols.

The proclamation that God is love is woven throughout the biblical narrative, from Genesis to Revelation. Some people think they see a vengeful God in the Old Testament and a loving God in the New Testament. To them, it's as if God had a personality change between the testaments. I don't think that's the case at all. In both testaments, God is consistently loving, though sometimes quite scary.

Calvinists and others stress the sovereignty of God, but then they look to humans for models of sovereignty. Therefore, they imagine God as some surly human king writ large, like one of the monarchs in *Game of Thrones*, only bigger and meaner. Whereas, Wesley is clear, God expresses all divine powers through love and grace. Love is God's "reigning attribute," Wesley says, and it "sheds an amiable glory on all his other perfections."[3]

Wesley reminds us that not only are we created by a loving God; we are created in the *image* of our loving God. There is more to the story, of course. That image has become corrupted, and restoring it in us is the aim of God's human rescue project. But the corruption of God's image is not foundational. It's the cause of the human predicament, but it's not the deepest truth about us. What's foundational is that all humans—even that clown down the street whom you despise for his filthy habits and nasty politics—*all humans* are created in God's loving image. The deepest truth about us is that we are created for loving relationship with God and one another.

---

3. New Testament Notes, 1 John 4:8.

The key for Wesley is 1 John 4.19: "We love because God first loved us."

God cares for each of us. God wants a relationship with each of us. And so God reaches out to us in our brokenness and calls us to Jesus. In Jesus, God shows us what love is like and what we should be like. Because we are loved, we are able to love ourselves and to love others. God's love changes us. God's love heals us. God's love transforms us. God's love gives us the heart transplant we need to become truly human.

Biblically, your heart is the essential you—not only the center of your emotions but also the center of your will and character. So it is that Saint Augustine says, "You have made us for yourself, O Lord, and our hearts are restless until they rest in you."[4] When Wesley says, "Let thy religion be the religion of the heart,"[5] he's saying that you'll never find peace of mind or spirit until you have religion of the heart.

In our natural state, unchanged by God's love, we are locked in a deep sleep. We are unaware of who God is and who we are in relation to God. But God calls us to wake up. God says, "Awake, you who sleep! Know who I am and who you are. Come to me and be restored to your true self. Come to me and learn what it is like to become fully human."

John and Charles Wesley have several such awakenings in their lifetimes. We'll review them after a personal story of awakening from me.

THREE THINGS TO KNOW

On the evening of November 22, 1991, I was driving home through downtown Kansas City from the offices of *The Kansas City Star*, where I worked as a copy editor. I was passing through a major intersection when a large sedan sped through a red light and hit the side of my little compact car just behind the driver's seat. The

---

4. *Confessions*, 1, 1.5.
5. Sermon 25, Sermon on Mount 5, 13, Works 5:326.

impact spun my car totally around. I was wearing a seat belt, but it didn't stop my head from striking the side door frame of the car.

I have no memory of the crash or of much else that happened that night. Linda says she received a call from police telling her that I had been injured but refused treatment—how smart was that?—so could she please come get me and take me to a hospital. The doctors concluded that I had a concussion and I would need to be under observation overnight. I was acting pretty goofy all this time, I'm told, but I don't remember anything about that.

Here is what I *do* remember.

I was asleep, and a nurse woke me up and shined a light in my eyes and poked me in several places and asked several strange questions and said she'd be back in an hour to do it again.

I realized that I was in a hospital and that I hurt just about everywhere, but my head hurt the most. I wondered what could have happened to put me in such a state. I couldn't remember anything. I wondered what I might have been doing *before* whatever happened to put me in such a state, and I couldn't remember that either. In fact, I couldn't remember *anything*. I couldn't remember my name. I couldn't remember the name of a single person I knew. I couldn't remember who I was, what I did for a living, whether I was married, whether I had children. I couldn't remember *anything*.

It was the scariest feeling I've ever had. When you have no sense of personal identity and you have no feeling of being connected to others, you are truly alone in the universe. You have nothing to hang onto. You are *nothing*.

I lay there for a long time, trying to remember, but nothing came. Eventually I fell asleep. Then the nurse woke me again, and as soon as she left, the panic returned. And so it went throughout the night—a little sleep, the nurse waking me, wondering how I had gotten there, the panic of knowing nothing.

It is likely that the nurse explained things to me each time she woke me up. But if she did, it did not register. I was wearing a hospital ID bracelet. Surely I could have looked at that and at least learned my name. But I don't remember ever doing so, and if I did, it didn't stick. All I remember is the disorientation and the panic. Who am I? Why am I here?

Finally, morning came. This time I woke on my own, and found a tray pushed close to my bed with breakfast on it. It was liquid breakfast, but food anyway. As I started to eat, I noticed two notes on the tray.

The first note was unsigned. I later learned that it was left by Linda and a close friend. It said: "Jim—You were in a car accident coming home from work tonight—Friday, Nov. 22. You have a concussion and are at Shawnee Mission."

So now I had a name and a story.

The second card was a prayer card provided by Shawnee Mission Medical Center in Overland Park, Kansas. The hospital, now called Advent Health, is run by Seventh Day Adventists. The prayer card contained Psalm 139. I immediately recognized it as one of my favorite psalms. "Lord, you have searched me and known me. You know when I sit down and when I rise up . . Even before a word is on my tongue, you know it . . . Where can I hide from your presence?"

You cannot appreciate what finding those two cards meant to me. I wept with joy. It was the first of many times I would weep in coming days. Every time I saw a familiar face, parts of my memory would come rushing back, as if I were meeting for the first time someone I had known all my life.

Those two cards told me three very important things. They told me that I was somebody, and that somebody loved me, and that God loved me.

I still didn't know who I was or to whom I was married or whether I had children or what I did for a living, but I did know those three things: I was somebody, I was loved by somebody, and I was loved by God.

And from there I was able to begin putting my memory back together. Knowing those three things, I was able to remember. Knowing those three things, I was re-membered as body and spirit were knit back together again. Knowing those three things was the beginning of my physical and mental healing—and that healing marked a turning in my life, for it had a strong spiritual dimension as well, and eventually it led me to pursue ordained ministry in the United Methodist Church.

May I suggest to you that knowing those three things is also the beginning of new life with God? May I suggest that knowing those three things might also be key to your identity and your purpose in living?

René Descartes was wrong. You need to know more than that you merely exist. You need to know *who you are.*

Who are you? You are somebody. You are loved by somebody. You are loved by God. Awake, you who sleep! Never forget *who* you are. Never forget *whose* you are. Come to God and be restored to who you really are!

AWAKENINGS

Despite its name, Christ Church College is more secular than religious when the Wesley brothers are educated there. John manages to maintain the childhood faith that got him through Charterhouse School. He places his hope for salvation on three things: "1. Not being so bad as other people. 2. Having still a kindness for religion. And, 3. Reading the Bible, going to church, and saying my prayers."[6] Yet, he realizes later, "during that whole time I had no more of the love of God than a stone."[7]

Looking back, he sees that God always works in his life "by degrees."[8] Starting in 1725, several events change the trajectory of his life by many degrees. If repentance and conversion are matters of turning to a new way, he repents and is converted many times in his lifetime. His is a life of continual reawakening and renewal.

Wesley is never specific about what causes him to turn in 1725. He is about twenty-two and ready to complete his undergraduate work when his parents—especially his father—begin to

---

6. Journal, May 24, 1738, 2, Works 1:98.
7. "Letter to the Bishop of London," I, Works 8:488.
8. Journal, Aug. 8, 1738, Works 1:135.

press him to seek holy orders. Dad thinks son would make a fine country parson. Son prefers an academic career. But for a time their plans run parallel, because ordination is required for an Oxford teaching fellowship.

Whatever the specific cause, Wesley is awakened to his sad spiritual state. Where before he was pretty much ignorant of God, now "it pleased God to give me a settled resolution to be, not a nominal, but a real Christian."[9] He is directed, by "the providence of God," to read two books that change his outlook on life. The first is *The Christian Pattern*, a new paraphrase of the Thomas à Kempis classic *The Imitation of Christ* prepared by George Stanhope, dean of Canterbury Cathedral.

"The nature and extent of inward religion, the religion of the heart, now appeared to me in a stronger light than ever it had done before," Wesley says.[10] He sees that he must give all his heart to God, not just part of it. Therefore, he begins to "aim at and pray for inward holiness."[11]

Helping to focus his aim is another book, *Rule and Exercises of Holy Living and Dying* by Jeremy Taylor. He's an Anglican royalist who was persecuted by the roundheads during the civil war nearly a century before. Wesley is especially moved by Taylor's emphasis on purity of intention. "Instantly I resolved to dedicate all my life to God—all my thoughts, and words, and actions; being thoroughly convinced, there was no medium; but that every part of my life (not some only) must either be a sacrifice to God, or myself, that is, in effect, to the devil."[12]

Later, both he and Charles will be moved by two books by the defrocked but still influential Anglican mystic William Law. You can catch the tone of the books from their titles: *A Serious Call to a Devout and Holy Life* and *A Practical Treatise on Christian Perfection.* The poet Samuel Johnson, a friend of John's, said the first

---

9. Sermon 81, "In What Sense Are We to Leave the World," 23, Works 6:473.

10. "Plain Account of Christian Perfection," 3, Works 11:366–67.

11. Journal, May 24,1738, Works: 1:99.

12. "Plain Account of Christian Perfection," 2, Works 11:366.

book turned his life around, so it's no wonder the Wesley brothers feel so great a spiritual debt to Law.

Now convinced "of the absolute impossibility of being half a Christian,"[13] Wesley begins to rigorously follow the spiritual disciplines of fasting, prayer, self-examination, and receiving Holy Communion. He's so serious—and so anxious—about his progress that he records his inner journey in a red notebook that once belonged to his Puritan grandfather, John Westley (after whom he was named, though Samuel Wesley changed the spelling of his last name to distance himself from his father). He devises his own code (unbroken for many years after his death) to record meticulous notes on his spiritual progress. Keeping a diary in code may sound bizarre to us today, but apparently it was a common practice at the time. Charles later adopts it as well.

Despite all his efforts, Wesley feels as far from God as ever. Several years later, preaching to his peers at St. Mary's Church in Oxford, he humbles himself before them. "I declare my own folly upon the house-top, for yours and the gospel's sake," he says. "All this time I was but almost a Christian."[14]

Even as he struggles spiritually, he advances in other ways. He completes his master's degree and is ordained as a priest. He is elected a fellow at Oxford's Lincoln College, an academic status that guarantees him a modest but steady income for many years. He also gets practical ministry experience serving for two years as his father's curate in the hamlet of Wroot, not far from Epworth.

Then he gets a request from Charles, who has begun his studies at Christ Church. Freed from the constraints of Westminster School, Charles is afraid he'll turn into a party animal. He starts a study group with other students who are serious about their academic and religious growth. He invites John to come lead it. Under John's guidance, the group grows to fifteen and gradually moves away from academics to an almost exclusively spiritual focus. They meet several nights each week for study and prayer; they fast two days a week; they hold one another accountable for spiritual

13. "Plain Account of Christian Perfection," I.4, Works 11:367.
14. Sermon 2, "Almost Christian," I.12–13, Works 5:21.

growth; and they engage in such social activism as helping the poor and visiting those who are sick or imprisoned. They also receive holy communion once a week, an act that fellow students deride as "popery"—a nasty charge in the fiercely anti-Catholic temper of the time in England.

"Sacramentarians" is just one of the scornful names the group acquires. Others are Enthusiasts, the Godly Club, and the Holy Club. They're also called *Methodists* because they follow a demanding method. John does not like the nickname at first, but eventually he warms to it. Looking back, he calls the Oxford group the "first rise of Methodism."[15] These are men who want to be "downright Bible Christians," he says.[16] Indeed, several go on to play major roles not only in the Methodist Revival but also in the hierarchy of the Church of England.

In the spring of 1735, Samuel Wesley dies at age 73. John has served in his father's place for several months, and he's now told that the Epworth position is his if he wants it. He declines because he still prefers an academic career, and he wants to continue the Oxford Methodist experiment, if only for his own spiritual health. Then another, more surprising offer comes: How would he like to lead some of his Methodists on a mission to Georgia in the American colonies?

John is eager to try his Methodist experiment on new ground. As a "High Church" Anglican, he believes in adhering as closely as possible to the theology and practices of the early Christian church. The rough American wilderness is surely the perfect laboratory for exploring how to restore apostolic Christianity. John is especially enthusiastic about the prospect of ministering to Native Americans. "I hope to learn the true sense of the Gospel of Christ by preaching to the heathen," he tells one of his sponsors.[17]

Charles is more skeptical. Organizers of the trip want him to be ordained as well as John, and he's not at all sure he wants to be a priest. But John insists, and Charles is fast-tracked to priesthood.

15. "A Short History of the People Called Methodists," 9, Works 13:307.

16. "A History of Methodism," 6, Works 8:348.

17. Oct. 10, 1735 letter to "a friend," (John Burton), Works 12:38.

By the end of October he and John and two other Oxford Methodists are on a ship bound for Georgia.

It takes more than four months to get there, including two months at open sea. The tedium of the voyage is relieved by several violent storms. John is amazed that some of the other passengers show no fear. These are Moravians, twenty-six members of a Pietist Lutheran sect from Germany who also are going to America as missionaries. Where he and the Oxford Methodists are cowering against the wind and waves, the Moravians are calmly singing psalms. John is ashamed of his fear. He wants the same faith-filled assurance that the Moravians have. In conversations with him, they are eager to offer him "a more excellent way" of following Jesus—justification by grace through faith rather than by moral striving. He is entranced—even though he must realize, somewhere in the back of his head, that the Church of England has always insisted that justification comes through faith, not works.

Georgia does not live up to expectations. The colony is primitive enough—only three years old—but the few Indians they encounter are not interested in hearing about Jesus. John becomes parish minister to the settlers in and around Savannah. Charles is assigned to Frederica, a rude settlement one hundred miles to the south. His primary duty is to act as personal secretary to the colony's governor—a position he has no aptitude for.

Many of the rough colonists in Savannah do not take well to John's High Church ways. Still, he is able to establish a religious society patterned after the Oxford Methodists. The society is successful enough that he later views this experience as the second rise of Methodism.[18] After barely surviving one winter sleeping on the cold floor of a tent, Charles gives up. Feverish and racked by dysentery, he has to be carried on board the ship that takes him home. John stays and thrives. He even courts a comely young woman named Sophy Hopkey. But she tires of his romantic blunders and marries another. When he publicly shames her, months of misunderstanding and resentment boil over, and the wrath of

---

18. "A Short History of the People Called Methodists," 9, Works 13:307.

the colony lands on him hard. Under threat of arrest, he slips away in the night and catches a ship bound for home.

"I went to America to convert the Indians; but O! who shall convert me?" he laments. "I have a fair summer religion. I can talk well—nay, and believe myself, while no danger is near. But let death look me in the face, and my spirit is troubled."[19]

Reunited at home, the discouraged brothers soon begin meeting weekly with some Moravians on Fetter Lane in London. The Moravians seem to have what they need spiritually. Peter Boehler, a young Moravian whom Charles is tutoring in English, becomes their spiritual tutor (as he will to many others later as a Moravian bishop). John later sees the formation of this religious society as the third rise of Methodism.[20]

"The faith I want," John declares, "is a sure trust and confidence in God, that, through the merits of Christ, my sins are forgiven and I am reconciled to the favor of God."[21] Under Boehler's guidance, he resolves to renounce "all dependence, in whole or in part, upon my own works or righteousness, on which I had grounded my hope of salvation, though I knew it not, from my youth up."[22] Still, after years of living as a legalistic perfectionist, it's not easy for him to change.

Since returning from America, both brothers have preached salvation by faith alone and have been booted out of several churches. John wonders if he should quit preaching it at all, if only because he has so little faith himself. Boehler tells him: "Preach faith till you have it, and then, because you *have* it, you will preach faith."[23] Fake it until you make it? Not exactly. The brothers already *have* faith, of one degree or another; they just can't *feel* it. They have an *intellectual* but not an *experiential* knowledge of faith. What they need is some blessed assurance that their faith is genuine. They find it in May of 1738.

19. Journal, Jan. 24, 1738, Works 1:74.

20. "A Short History of the People Called Methodists," 9, Works 13:307.

21. Journal addition to Feb. 29, 1738, Works 1:77.

22. Journal May 24, 1738, Works 1:102.

23. Journal March 4, 1738; Works 1:86.

Charles is first. Since early February he has suffered a bad bout of pleurisy. He appears so close to death on March 2 that John is summoned from Oxford to his bedside. It happens again in late May. On the morning of May 21, Pentecost Sunday, Charles fears that he is about to die, and he gives himself up to God's keeping. He's apparently in a state of delirium when he hears someone come into his room and say, "In the name of Jesus of Nazareth, arise, and believe, and thou shalt be healed of all thy infirmities." It's similar to a message he received a few days before while reading Martin Luther's commentary on the book of Galatians. He feels "a strange palpitation of heart," and though he fears to say it, he says, "I believe! I believe!" And he affirms, "I now found myself at peace with God, and rejoiced in hope of loving Christ."[24]

John has a similar experience on May 24, when a friend invites him to join a Moravian group meeting in London. His description of the event is legendary:

> In the evening I went very unwillingly to a society in Aldersgate Street, where one was reading Luther's Preface to the Epistle to the Romans. About a quarter before nine, while he was describing the change which God works in the heart through faith in Christ, I felt my heart strangely warmed. I felt I did trust in Christ, Christ alone for salvation, and an assurance was given me that he had taken away my sins, even mine, and saved me from the law of sin and death.[25]

When he visits Charles later that night, he also declares, "I believe!"[26]

Clearly these events are milestones in the life of both brothers, major points of turning and spiritual renewal. But what do we *call* them? They're often labeled "conversion" experiences. Indeed, that's how Charles refers to his experience at least once.[27] But what are they converted *from* and *to*? It's too glib (and in many cases, quite

24. Charles Wesley Journal, May 21, 1738.

25. John Wesley Journal May 24, 1738, Works 1:103.

26. Kimbrough and Newport *Manuscript Journal,* 1:111.

27. Charles Wesley Journal, May 23, 1738.

self-serving) to say that they are converted from a spiritually arid establishment or "mainline" faith to spiritually alive "evangelical" faith. Though clearly both brothers join the ranks of eighteenth-century evangelicals, they remain loyal priests of the Church of England who are committed to a High Church understanding of Scripture and worship. *What* they *believe* is unchanged; what's new is how they feel moved to *express* it.

When Charles declares, "I believe," *what* does he now believe that he didn't believe before? Yes, he believes that God's grace saves him through faith alone. That's nothing new; it's standard Anglican doctrine. Surely he believed it before. What Charles *believes* now that he didn't before is that God's grace actually saves *Charles Wesley* by grace though faith alone. Perhaps for the first time, it's *personal* for him. As he says in the original verse 5 of "O For a Thousand Tongues to Sing," he truly believes to the depth of his being that "me he loved, the Son of God; for me, for me he died!"[28] Similarly, John suddenly feels that God has acted in *his* life and "taken away my sins, *even mine.*"

In John's case it especially appears to be heart and head finally coming together; experiential reinforcing intellectual understanding, trust in the person of Christ replacing mere assent to the truth about Christ. Receiving full assurance of his salvation, he is "converted" from nominal faith to genuine faith. He moves "from faith to faith," from an earnest "almost Christian" to the "altogether Christian" he has wanted to be since 1725.

One way of illustrating the change is noting a difference in motivation. Before Aldersgate, Wesley is self-absorbed and often quite selfish. After Aldersgate, he is much more open to attending to the needs of others above his own. It's as if the experience helped free him from his false self so that he could become his true self.

He may also have moved from the "faith of a servant" to the "faith of a son." Both are forms of saving faith (or so I read him; he is hard to follow on this point, and scholars are not united in interpreting him). But where a servant responds to God out of fear and obligation, a son responds fully out of love. A son (or daughter;

28. "O For A Thousand Tongues To Sing."

"son" is a royal title, not a sex designation) is brought into the family of God as a child of God. The child receives assurance of the Holy Spirit dwelling within, thus enabled to live with childlike confidence in God.[29] In modern terms, it might be expressed as the difference between being merely "saved" and experiencing the full fruits of salvation. The first is a step toward the second that all are expected to complete. Though taking that step may go beyond the bare minimum "necessary" for salvation, it brings you closer to perfection in love in the here and now—and perfection in love is what it's all about anyway.[30]

Both brothers continue to have periods of doubt and uncertainty even after these experiences of awakening. Indeed, John will soon claim that he is *not* and *never has been* a real Christian.[31] Still, neither one of the Wesleys is remotely the same afterward. If God works in their lives "by degrees," the compass continues to spin wildly even after May 1738. More moments of turning and "conversion" are ahead.

HYMNS OF LIBERATION

"And Can It Be" is one of two hymns that Charles Wesley is thought to have written shortly following his Pentecost experience in May 1738. It was originally titled "Free Grace."[32]

And Can It Be That I Should Gain

1. And can it be that I should gain an interest in the Savior's blood?
Died he for me, who caused his pain, for me, who him to death pursued?
Amazing love! How can it be that thou, my God, shouldst die for me?

---

29. Sermon 106, "On Faith," 10–12, Works 7:198–200.
30. Sermon 110, "On the Discoveries of Faith," 13–14, Works 7:236.
31. Journal Jan. 4, 1739, Works 1:170.
32. "And Can It Be That I Should Gain."

2 'Tis mystery all! Th'Immortal dies! Who can explore his strange design?

In vain the firstborn seraph tries to sound the depths of love divine!

'Tis mercy all! Let earth adore, let angel minds inquire no more.

3. He left his Father's throne above, so free, so infinite his grace.

Emptied himself of all but love and bled for Adam's helpless race.

'Tis mercy all, immense and free, for O my God, it found out me!

4. Long my imprisoned spirit lay, fast bound in sin and nature's night.

Thine eye diffused a quickening ray. I woke, the dungeon flamed with light.

My chains fell off, my heart was free. I rose, went forth, and followed thee.

5. No condemnation now I dread. Jesus, and all in him, is mine.

Alive in him, my living Head, and clothed in righteousness divine.

Bold I approach the eternal throne, and claim the crown, through Christ my own.

The second hymn is "Where Shall My Wondering Soul Begin?"[33] Its language is sometimes difficult, and it is considerably less popular than "And Can It Be?"

Where Shall My Wondering Soul Begin?

1. Where shall my wondering soul begin? How shall I all to heaven aspire?

A slave redeemed from death and sin, a brand plucked from eternal fire,

how shall I equal triumphs raise, or sing my great deliverer's praise?

2. O how shall I the goodness tell, Father, which thou to me hast showed?

That I, a child of wrath and hell, I should be called a child of God!

33. Holzemer, "Where Shall My Wondering Soul Begin."

Should know, should feel my sins forgiven, blest with this foretaste of heaven!

The original has "antepast," instead of "foretaste." (Antepast? *Really?*) It continues for six more sometimes dense verses.

Though not directly connected to the events of May 1738, the 1742 hymn "Depth of Mercy" also seems appropriate here.[34]

Depth of Mercy

1. Depth of mercy! Can there be mercy still reserved for me?
Can my God his wrath forbear? Me, the chief of sinners, spare?
2. I have long withstood his grace, long provoked him to his face;
would not hearken to his calls; grieved him by a thousand falls.
3. I my Master have denied, I afresh have crucified;
oft profaned his hallowed name, put him to an open shame.
4. There for me the Savior stands, shows his wounds and spreads his hands:
God is love! I know, I feel; Jesus weeps, but loves me still!
5. Now incline me to repent! Let me now my fall lament!
Now my foul revolt deplore! Weep, believe, and sin no more.

SIX GOOD QUESTIONS . . . TO CONSIDER OR DISCUSS

1. What kind of God do you worship?

2. Have you ever lost sense of who you are? How did you return to yourself?

3. John Wesley sees God working in his life by "degrees." Is this your experience?

4. Do you ever feel "the providence of God" guiding your reading or other actions?

34. "History of Hymns: 'Depth of Mercy.'"

5. Wesley says you can't be "almost" a Christian—either you are or you aren't. Are you "all in" for Jesus?

6. Have you ever had a conversion experience similar to the ones reported by the Wesley brothers?

Six Great Sermons, #2

"Original Sin," Sermon 44, from 1759: "Know your disease! Know your cure!"

3

No Matter What

Cynics contend that only one piece of Christian doctrine can be empirically proved, and that involves the doctrine of sin. Even atheists can agree with the apostle Paul when he says, "There is no one who is righteous, not even one" (Rom 3:10).

If you doubt this, look around. You'll see evidence everywhere—on TV, in your newspaper, in social media, in your neighborhood, in your daily relationships. The world is seriously messed up. People don't behave well. Things are not right. Things are not the way they're supposed to be.

"Not the way they're supposed to be"—that's a great definition of sin from contemporary theologian Cornelius Plantinga.[1] He's a Calvinist, and therefore perhaps an unlikely ally of John Wesley, but I think they would get along pretty well here. God wants people to live in shalom, in loving relationship. That's the way things are *supposed* to be. But that's not the way they *are*. Something has gone horribly wrong. We call this wrong "sin."

How horribly wrong are things? Wesley says sin is a voluntary breach of the law of love,[2] that "great, unchangeable law of love, the holy love of God and our neighbor."[3] Sin is more than a

1. Plantinga, *Not the Way*.

2. Letter to Elizabeth Bennis, one of his sisters, June 16, 1772; Works 12:394.

3. Sermon 5, "Justification by Faith," IV.1, Works 5:60.

few things we get wrong. It's a state of being. It's a matrix of action and reaction in which we appear hopelessly trapped. So trapped are we that although our actions may sometimes have positive motive and positive effect, too much of the time they arise from negative motive and have harmful effect. As one observer puts it, it's as if the entire human family has some sort of factory defect that prevents us from functioning properly.

James, the brother of Jesus, pinpoints the problem in the letter that bears his name: "Those conflicts and disputes among you, where do they come from? Do they not come from your cravings that are at war within you? You want something and do not have it; so you commit murder. And you covet something and cannot obtain it; so you engage in disputes and conflicts" (Jas 4:1–2).

Even the apostle Paul admits: "I do not understand my own actions. For I do not do what I want, but I do the very thing I hate. . . . I can *will* what is right, but I cannot *do* it" (Rom 7:16, 18).

Something within us is terribly broken. We are willing to commit awful acts to get what we desire. Comedian and filmmaker Woody Allen was once caught in a messy scandal and he explained: "The heart wants what the heart wants. There's no logic to these things." (Did he know he was quoting Emily Dickinson— and did *she* know she was quoting Blaise Pascal in *Pensées*?)

Trying *not* to sin is like holding your breath. You can do it for only so long. An addiction counselor once told me, "Telling an addict to stop using drugs is like telling someone with the flu to stop throwing up." Sin is a kind of addiction. Telling a sinner to stop sinning is like telling someone with the flu to stop throwing up. But this is not the kind of sickness you get over in 24 hours, or 48 hours, or 4,800 hours.

No wonder Paul exclaims: "Wretched man that I am! Who will rescue me from this body of death?" But then he answers his own question (Rom 7:24–25): "Thanks be to God through Jesus Christ our Lord!"

At its core, Wesleyan spirituality is about salvation. Sin and its effects are what we need to be saved from. In chapter two we talked about needing to know who we are. The deepest truth about us is that we are created in the loving image of God. But that's not all there is to our story. In his great hymn, "Love Divine, All Loves Excelling," Charles Wesley says we have become "bent to sinning." Though we are created in God's loving image, that image has gotten bent and misshapen—distorted the way a funhouse mirror distorts what you see in it, the way a broken mirror presents a fragmented picture of things, the way a dirty mirror shows only a smudged reflection of what's there.

Sin is an infection of human nature, John Wesley says. This infection has spread itself over the whole person, "leaving no part uninfected."[4] And it's an infection that will prove *fatal*.[5] What can be done about it? Wesley says: "Know your disease! Know your cure! You were born in sin; therefore, 'you must be born again,' born of God. By nature you are corrupted; by grace you shall be wholly renewed."[6]

Viewing sin as a disease puts the idea of salvation in a new light from what we may be accustomed to. John Calvin, a lawyer, views everything in legal terms, so it's no wonder he has a forensic view of salvation. You disobey, you must pay. Thanks to his reading in early Eastern theologians, Wesley thinks in more therapeutic terms. His main concern is not prosecution and pardon but healing. "The proper nature of religion, of the religion of Jesus Christ," he says, "is God's method of healing a soul which is diseased. Hereby the Great Physician of souls applies medicine to heal this sickness, to restore human nature" to its original design and "renew our hearts in the image of God."[7]

You don't go to a physician unless you're sick, and you don't go to the Great Physician unless you know you are a sinner, Wesley says.[8] The process begins with repentance, which Wesley also calls self-knowledge. You have to recognize who you are before you can change. Once you realize who you are, and what you have become

4. New Testament Notes, Rom 6:6.

5. Sermon 44, "Original Sin," II.11, Works 6:62.

6. Sermon 44, "Original Sin," III.5, Works 6:65.

7. Sermon 44, "Original Sin," III.3, Works 6:64.

8. "Doctrine of Original Sin," Part III, Works 9:315

because of sin, you will want to change because the Holy Spirit is working in your heart to spark such desire for change. We've almost worn out the word "repent" with poor usage. Basically, it means to turn from one way and go another. It means recognizing that you've been going the wrong way.

"Repent, that is, know yourselves," Wesley says. "Awake, then, thou that sleepest. Know thyself to be a sinner, and what manner of sinner thou art. Know that corruption of thy inmost nature, whereby thou art very far gone from original righteousness . . . Know that thou are corrupted in every power, in every faculty of thy soul; that thou art totally corrupted in every one of these, all the foundations being out of course."[9]

The cause of our corruption is "original sin"—that is, the sin of disobedience committed by Adam and Eve in the Garden of Eden. Some theologians insist that their guilt is passed on to us in some way. Yes, Wesley says, we inherit the *consequence* of their sin; but no, we do not inherit any *guilt* from it. That guilt is "cancelled by the righteousness of Christ" when each of us is born, so the only guilt we need to worry about is guilt for our own sins.[10] As if that were not enough burden to carry!

So diseased are we that we are not capable of healing ourselves. We need to wake up because we are so far gone that we're spiritually asleep. Happily, God offers a cure for our disease. God wants to save us. God reaches way down to pull us up out of our predicament.

John 3:16 says: "God so loved the world that he gave his only Son, so that whoever trusts him may not perish but have eternal life." You may have been taught that God hates your lousy guts because you're a miserable sinner. You're nothing but a vile worm, and you deserve to roast on a spit in the fires of hell for the next six bazillion years. I have a news flash for you—a bit of gospel news. *God does not hate you.* Never has. Never will. God does not hate *anyone.* God so loves you and everyone else that God was willing

---

9. Sermon 7, "Way to the Kingdom," II.1, Works 5:81–82.

10. "Predestination Calmly Considered," 34, Works 10:223; Letter to John Mason.

to step down into our mess and take the worst we could deliver, even death on a cross. But God won't accept our rejection. God won't let sin have the final word. God is intent on saving us—and saving the rest of God's good creation as well. God wants to restore creation to its original intent and, out of "abounding grace," to give humans a "far higher blessing by Christ that they lost by Adam"[11] and a similar blessing to "the whole brute creation."[12]

God wants not only to forgive us for causing great hurt by our sin. God wants to rescue us from sin altogether. God wants to remake us in God's very own image, to rebuild us from head to toe according to the original blueprint. That means we end up *looking* just like Jesus, who is the spitting image of God, and also *acting* just like Jesus because we have the same mind as Jesus because the Holy Spirit lives within us and is constantly renewing us.[13]

That renewal can take a lifetime, so salvation is the journey of a lifetime. Along the way, we continue to struggle. We are no longer captive to sin, but we are hardly far from free of its influence, around us and in us as well.

In many churches today, sin has a peculiar definition. Sin is something *other people* do. Specifically, sin is what other people do that you don't *like* to do. By that definition, sin has everything to do with personal preference, very little to do with treating people right, and hardly anything to do with God. It's all about overlooking your own sin while focusing on the sins of those who sin *differently* than you do.

For example, many churches fulminate against homosexuality, though Jesus never mentioned it, and ignore divorce, which Jesus condemned. I am OK with our acceptance of divorce as a tragic necessity in our messy lives. But if we can find ways to accept divorce even when Jesus didn't, why can't we accept homosexuality, about which Jesus never said a word? The way we Christians split hairs on such things, it's no wonder we are so widely known

11. "Doctrine of Original Sin," II I.14, Works 9:253. See also Sermon 59, "God's Love to Fallen Man," 3–4 Works 6:232.

12. Sermon 60, "General Deliverance," III.3, Works 6:249.

13. Phil 2:5; Rom 12:2; 1 Cor 2:16.

as hypocrites. (I am aware that passages outside the four Gospels, principally the well-known "clobber" passages, can be mustered to condemn homosexual behavior. I also am aware of linguistic and cultural issues that make strict interpretation of these passages highly problematic. Obviously, the subject is too large to explore more deeply here.)

I have told you before that I grew up in a fundamentalist church. Let me tell you a little more about it.

Being an usher in that church was a big deal for men—and all the ushers were men, of course. Ushers had two duties. They handed out bulletins at the start of the service, and they collected the offering at the end of the service. In between, they stood outside the side entrance and smoked cigarettes.

Because they were outside, they missed the pastor fulminating about the evils of tobacco and alcohol and movies and cards and dancing and anything else that might vaguely resemble fun. When the ushers came down the aisle to collect the offering or bring it forward, you didn't have to look to *see* them coming; you could *smell* them coming. They reeked of cigarette smoke.

As far as I know, no one ever objected to the ushers standing outside sinning while other church members were singing God's praise. That was part of the deal. Some sins, by some people, were tolerated.

I remember one Sunday when the atmosphere in the church was simply electric. I didn't know what was going on until the pastor was halfway through his sermon and he started confessing his sins. Minor stuff at first, but finally he got to the big one. It seems that he was counseling this woman in his office one evening, and at the end of the session he thought they ought to get down on their knees on the floor for prayer, and soon he was taking off her clothes—hey, you know how these things go.

The pastor tearfully begged for forgiveness. The church graciously forgave him. But the woman he'd "counseled" this way? Why, they drove that shameless hussy right out of the church!

When I was a sophomore in high school, I had a hopeless crush on a girl in the youth group who was a senior. I thought she was the prettiest and smartest girl I'd ever met. Shortly after graduating from high school, she made two big mistakes. Her first big mistake was getting pregnant without getting married. When her boyfriend skipped town, she made her second big mistake. She looked to her church for support. Church women shamed her, made her feel like dirt, and drove her out.

Friends, this is not the way it's supposed to be. That's why we need a Savior, because even after our own sins have been forgiven, we can be cruel and unforgiving to others. We can be so cruel and unforgiving that maybe we've forgotten what we were like before we were forgiven. A rough-hewn friend of mine once said, with a big grin, "If you think I'm a jerk now, you should have seen me *before* I knew Jesus!" He knew he was still a work in progress, as are we all.

Some churches are all about preaching sin, and you can feel pretty beat up before you get out of there some Sunday mornings. But Cornelius Plantinga says the gospel is not about *sin.* The gospel is about the *cure* for sin. The gospel is about Jesus Christ. It is our privilege and our call as followers of Jesus to bear witness to him by the way we live. Theologian N. T. Wright says, "Our task, as image-bearing, God-loving, Christ-shaped, Spirit-filled Christians" is to announce redemption and healing to a world that desperately needs to hear such good news.[14]

So if you bear God's image—and I know you do—and if you love the Lord—I can't testify about that—and if you are being shaped in the image of Christ and you are filled with the Holy Spirit, I invite you to proclaim with me this gospel message to all those who need to hear it.

No matter who you are, God loves you.

No matter how beautiful or how handsome you are, God loves you.

No matter how young or how old you are, God loves you.

No matter how much money you have or don't have, God loves you.

No matter how big or small your house is, God loves you.

14. Wright, *Challenge of Easter,* 44.

No matter what kind of car you drive, God loves you.

No matter what race or nationality you are, God loves you.

No matter what language you speak, God loves you.

No matter what culture you came from, God loves you.

No matter who your parents are, God loves you.

No matter who your children are, God loves you.

No matter how smart you are, God loves you.

No matter how much schooling you have, God loves you.

No matter your shoe size, your hat size or your ego size, God loves you.

No matter what sex you are, God loves you.

No matter what sex you *were*, God loves you.

No matter what your sexual orientation, God loves you.

No matter how many mistakes you've made, God loves you.

No matter how much good you've done, God loves you.

No matter how much bad you've done, God loves you.

No matter how many people you've helped, God loves you.

No matter how many people you've hurt, God loves you.

No matter what you think of God, God loves you.

No matter *what*, God loves you.

No matter what, God wants to save you from sin and its ultimate consequences—and God *will*, if you'll allow it. Oh, yes, God will!

Would you pray this prayer with me?

> *O Lord our God, we confess to you and to one another that we are not the loving persons you created us to be. We regret the hurt and pain that our unloving ways have caused you and others. Forgive us our sins as we forgive those who have sinned against us. Create within us a new heart, O God—a heart that beats with your love for all. Then remake us in the loving image in which we were created—your image, O Lord, the image of Jesus, our Savior and our Lord, in whose name we pray. Amen.*

A DISPOSITION OF THE HEART

With repentance and faith, we move closer to the heart of Wesleyan theology. Let's return to that formulation that I offered earlier.

> **God's love** is revealed by **grace.**
> It sparks **repentance** and inspires **faith.**
> It ignites **rebirth** and animates **holiness,**
> *creating* **happiness.**

In the next chapter, we'll focus on God's love and grace. For now, let's concentrate on repentance and faith.

For the longest time, I wondered why we must repent before we believe. Wouldn't you think it should be the other way around? Don't we have to trust in God *before* we decide to turn our lives around and go God's way rather than our own? Even if we're sure we're lost, don't we need to know a better route before we set out on it?

First, note that when Jesus begins his mission in Galilee, this is his message: "The time is fulfilled, and the kingdom of God has come near. Repent and believe the good news!" (Mark 1:15). Repentance comes first for Jesus. We have to repent *before* we can trust the good news he embodies.

That's because, as John Wesley explains, repentance is "an inward change, a change of mind."[15] To repent means to change your heart and mind so that you can become more the person God intends you to be. It means to turn, to go another way, to change course. We likely repent many times in a lifetime, sometimes making big course corrections, sometimes smaller ones. The initial course correction is always the biggest because it's "a change of mind from sin to holiness."[16]

We have to recognize *who we are* before we can change. We have to quit lying to ourselves and face the truth. If I think, "I'm really a wonderful person," I have no reason to change. But if I realize, "I'm really not so wonderful after all, and I'm far below

15. Sermon 14, "Repentance of Believers," I.1, Works 5:157.
16. Sermon 14, "Repentance of Believers," I.1, Works 5:157.

God's estimation of who I should be," then I know that I have to change. I have to repent. Before we can discover our new self, who we are in Christ, we have to die to our old, false self.

We often associate repentance with guilt. Guilt may be a part of it, but it's not necessarily a large part of it, and preaching guilt is usually repulsive, not to mention non-productive. My favorite notation here comes from the book *City of God* by Sara Miles. She quotes Paul Fromberg, onetime rector of St. Gregory of Nyssa Episcopal Church in San Francisco, as saying: "Jesus doesn't care if you feel guilty. Jesus wants you to change."[17] See, feeling guilty is easy. Change is never easy, if only because it involves self-awareness and self-knowledge—and these are just about the last things most of us want to think about most of the time. Guilt gets us nowhere because guilt looks backwards. Repentance looks forward. Repentance opens us to God's new possibilities. It's a step toward God and away from sin.

"Real Christianity always begins in poverty of spirit," Wesley says.[18] "We must repent before we can believe the gospel. We must be cut off from dependence on ourselves before we can truly depend on Christ. We must cast away all confidence in our own righteousness, or we cannot have true confidence in his."[19]

This realization is one of the things that happens to Wesley on the way to his awakening at Aldersgate. He realizes that he has spent most of his life working for salvation based on his own righteousness—which is to say, based on nothing more than vain striving—rather than the rich righteousness of Jesus Christ.

Repentance rightly leads to faith. Wesley calls faith a "spiritual light" from the Holy Spirit that guides us from the life of darkness to repentance and salvation.[20] Faith, he insists, is not "a bare assent to the truth of the Bible, of the articles of our creed, or of all that is contained in the Old and New Testament. The devils believe this,

---

17. Miles, *City of God*, 20.
18. Sermon 21, "Sermon on the Mount 1," I.1, Works 5:252.
19. Sermon 20, "Lord Our Righteousness," II.11, Works: 5:241.
20. Sermon 43, "Scripture Way of Salvation," II.1, Works 6:46.

as well as I or thou! And yet they are devils still."[21] No, faith "is not a speculative, rational thing, a cold lifeless assent, a train of ideas in the head." Rather, it is "a disposition of the heart."[22] It is "a sure trust in the mercy of God, through Christ Jesus. It is confidence in a pardoning God."[23]

It is, says the post-Aldersgate Wesley, a *living* faith—that is, "a sure trust and confidence which a man hath in God that, by the merits of Christ, his sins are forgiven and he reconciled to the favor of God—whereof doth follow a loving heart, to obey his commandments."[24]

Of these things few Christians would dispute. However, the Wesley brothers are forced to battle two substantially different accounts of how you might follow a loving heart and obey God.

The first involves the Moravian Brethren. Though John and Charles are greatly impressed by some aspects of Moravian piety, especially their use of small groups, other aspects drive them crazy. John goes so far as to learn German so he can talk with the Moravians in their native language. He even travels to Austria to visit their leader, Count Nicolaus von Zinzendorf. But the Moravians insist on "quietism," or "stillness." That is, they take literally the command in Ps 46:10, "Be still, and know that I am God!" For them, that means waiting passively for God to anoint them with the Holy Spirit. They do not study the Scriptures or pray or use other spiritual disciplines for fear that doing so might show lack of trust in God.

The Wesleys have little patience with any form of idleness. They believe in "active waiting." For them, to wait on God means using time-honored spiritual disciplines to open themselves to the promises from God. By the summer of 1840, they have had enough. They quit the Fetter Lane Society, taking several like-minded members with them. As painful as this split is, another causes even more long-term heartache.

21. Sermon 7, "Way to the Kingdom," 1.10, Works 5:85.
22. Sermon 1, "Salvation by Faith," I.4, Works 5:9.
23. Sermon 7, "Way to the Kingdom," I.10, Works 5:85.
24. Sermon 2, "Almost Christian," III.5, Works 5:23.

John Wesley once declares Methodism a "hair's breadth from Calvinism."[25] That thin but significant difference is the role of divine grace in human life—and Wesley says Calvin's doctrine of predestination makes a mockery of God's grace. Calvin himself calls the idea of limited atonement a "dreadful decree."[26] As it's often spelled out, it means that from the dawn of time God granted salvation to a limited number of people, and there's nothing anyone can do to change the outcome. If you're going to be saved, you'll be saved no matter what you do because God has already decided your fate. If you're not going to be saved, there's nothing you can do about that either—because God has already decided your fate.

Wesley thinks this notion is simply an abomination, just another form of quietism in a clever new disguise. For one thing, it can lead to *antinomianism*—literally, being "against the law." In other words, it works against application of any moral code. If you're going to heaven no matter how you behave, where's your motivation to do good to anyone but yourself? Conversely, if you're bound for hell no matter what you do, why not raise hell while you've got the chance? Since you can't know which way you're bound until it's too late to change your behavior, what's the easiest choice?

It also negates the whole idea of holiness. If God is going to save you no matter what you do or don't do, your relationship with God is irrelevant. In fact, you don't even *need* a relationship with God because your ticket to heaven is already punched.

It also can weaken your motivation for evangelism. Some Calvinists preach to everyone because they can't know who is saved and who isn't. Wesley thinks that if predestination is true, all preaching is in vain. If it's already decided who's in and who's out, why preach to anybody? You can't change anything![27] It also destroys any motivation to pray. If everything is already decided, asking God for anything is a waste of time. God already knows what's going to happen, and that's that.

25. "John Wesley letter to John Newton."
26. Calvin, Institutes, 3:23.7.
27. Sermon 128, "Free Grace," 10, Works 7:376

It also destroys any notion of human freedom and any notion of divine justice. Wesley explains: "Now if man be capable of choosing good or evil, then he is a proper object of the justice of God, acquitting or condemning, rewarding or punishing. But otherwise he is not. A mere machine is not capable of being either acquitted or condemned."[28] In short, Wesley says predestination "represents God as worse than the devil—as both more false, more cruel, and more unjust."[29]

Wesley's support of universal rather than limited atonement is often called "Arminian" because it's similar to the thinking of Dutch theologian James Arminius (1560–1609). Strictly speaking, Wesley is not a follower of Arminius, but in 1778 he starts publishing *The Arminian Magazine*, dedicated to spreading an anti-Calvinist message. It's an uphill fight because Calvinism has been the default mode for most Protestants for 150 years. (Indeed, a mild form of predestination is even enshrined in Article 17 of the Church of England's Articles of Religion.) Wesley won't give in, though, and the result is that the Methodist Revival splits again, into two new branches—one Calvinist and one Arminian. And the Calvinist branch is led by someone who can preach rings around Wesley.

His name is George Whitefield (pronounced WHIT-field). The lives of Whitefield and Wesley run roughly parallel in many ways, but Wesley is far better known today because his evangelical movement goes global while Whitefield's movement leaves little formal legacy (something Whitefield himself realized when it was too late to do much about it). Where Wesley is remembered for his organizational skills, Whitefield is remembered for his oratory. Short, plump and cross-eyed, he is sometimes belittled as "Dr. Squintum." But thanks for some early experience in the theater, he has a well-trained voice that he knows how to project to the rafters and beyond, plus a fine-tuned sense of the dramatic that makes every sermon a bravura performance. David Garrick, a London actor, is reported to remark that Whitefield could make you weep

28. "Predestination Calmly Considered," 52, Works 10: 233–34.

29. Sermon 128, "Free Grace," 25, Works 7:382.

just by the way he pronounces the word "Mesopotamia." Preaching at revivals in America, he will captivate even Benjamin Franklin, who becomes a good friend even though the two share few spiritual concerns.

Whitefield first encounters the Wesleys when he comes to Pembroke College at Oxford. Charles befriends him, and he joins the Oxford Methodists. Convinced of his need to repent, he takes the Methodist discipline to unhealthy extremes. When finally he looks outside himself for help, he cries out, "I thirst! I thirst!" and he feels the load of sin lifted from him.[30] It's spring 1735, three years before the Wesley brothers have a similar awakening experience. They are thousands of miles apart for some of this time, yet surely they do find some time to talk, and surely his experience sets an example for what they might expect to happen to them.

Whitefield leads the Oxford Methodists while the brothers are in Georgia and—at John's invitation—sets out to join John there even as John is returning home. He stays in Georgia only a few months, planning to return soon to plant an orphanage there—a dream that Charles was never able to realize and Whitefield brings to reality only after years of effort. Back in England, he hopes to resume preaching in and around London, where he has become famous, if controversial. But now he finds himself mostly unwelcome in Anglican pulpits, both because he preaches salvation by faith and the flamboyant way he preaches it. Denied a pulpit in one church, he preaches instead in the churchyard—and discovers that he's pretty good at outdoor preaching. Soon he's leading a revival among the miners at Kingswood, a slum outside of Bristol. He invites the Wesleys to come see what he's accomplishing—and then asks them to take over while he returns to America.

"I could scarce reconcile myself at first to this strange way of preaching in the fields," John says, "having been all my life . . . so tenacious of every point relating to decency and order that I should have thought the saving of souls almost a sin if it had not been done in church."[31] Upon reflection, however, he concedes that

30. Belcher, *George Whitefield,* 31–32.
31. Journal, March 29, 1739, Works 1.185.

Jesus' Sermon on the Mount was "one pretty remarkable precedent of field preaching."[32]

So, as "a sudden expedient, a thing submitted to, rather than chosen,"[33] because he is not allowed to preach anywhere else, he joins the ranks of outdoor preachers. On April 2, 1739: "At four in the afternoon, I submitted to be more vile, and proclaimed in the highways the glad tidings of salvation, speaking from a little eminence in a ground adjoining to the city, to about three thousand people. The Scripture on which I spoke was this . . . 'The Spirit of the Lord is upon me, because he hath anointed me to preach the gospel to the poor.'"[34] Soon Charles also is preaching in the open.

John, at least, has felt primed for this time for several months, since the day he walked to Oxford while reading Jonathan Edwards' 1737 account of revival in Northhampton, Massachusetts, titled *A Faithful Narrative of the Surprising Work of God.* Surely, he remarks, quoting Ps 118:23, "This is the Lord's doing, and it is marvelous in our eyes."[35]

The miners at Kingswood are starved for spiritual nourishment. Parish boundaries haven't been adjusted in ages, and the Church of England barely acknowledges that some people exist. Day after day, the Wesley brothers draw thousands of listeners to their services in early morning and evening. The Methodist Revival takes off. As John puts it, "The word of God ran as fire among the stubble."[36]

Early revival gatherings are far from the frequently staid meetings you might encounter in most Anglican churches of the day. Here, both preacher and congregation freely express "enthusiasm." We may struggle today to read Wesley's sermons; they seem so dry and rigidly formatted. But neither of the Wesleys preaches from a manuscript. The versions we read today were edited for

32. Journal, April 1, 1739, Works 1.185.

33. "A Farther Appeal to Men of Reason and Religion," VI.4, Works 8:113.

34. Journal, April 1, 1739, Works 1.185.

35. Journal Oct. 9. 1738, Works 1:160.

36. "Principles of a Methodist Farther Explained" (second letter to Thomas Church), June 17, 1746, VI.1.1, Works 8:468–69.

publication, not preaching. In the pulpit (even when there is no pulpit), the Wesleys may follow a careful outline, but they are animated, emotional, even fiery. And the response is often wild. Convicted of their sins, some people react hysterically. Cut to the heart, they burst into tears, shriek, and writhe in convulsions. "They dropped on every side as thunderstruck," John recalls of one early meeting. "One was so wounded by the sword of the Spirit that you would have imagined she could not live a moment." But soon she is singing God's praise.[37]

Looking back forty years later, John says that salvation by grace was their constant theme:

> It was our daily subject, both in verse and prose, and we vehemently defended it against all mankind. But in doing this we met with abundance of difficulty. We were assaulted and abused on every side. We were everywhere represented as mad dogs and treated accordingly. We were stoned in the streets, and several times narrowly escaped with our lives. In sermons, newspapers, and pamphlets of all kinds, we were painted as unheard-of monsters. But this moved us not. We went on, by the help of God, testifying salvation by faith both to small and great, and not counting our lives dear unto ourselves, so we might finish our course with joy.[38]

The threats to roving Methodist preachers are many and serious. Overland travel is difficult enough because of bad roads, bad weather, and bandits. But the reception they receive in many towns is often hostile. Simply by showing up to preach, they are disturbing the peace. Church and crown are nearly identical in many minds, so that any deviance from normal religious practice is a challenge to both church and state. "Your preaching frightens people out of their wits!" exclaims one critic.[39]

Crowds are often provoked by agitators hired by local clergy who resent the intrusion on their turf. Friendly listeners soon turn

---

37. Journal April 26, 1739; Works 1:188–89)
38. "Thoughts on Salvation by Faith," 1–2, Works 11:402–3.
39. Journal June 5, 1739, Works 1:199.

into angry mobs armed with refuse, rocks, and clubs. John and Charles are several times swept up in riots and narrowly escape death. The worst happens in 1741 at Hay-on-Wye in Wales when itinerant preacher William Seward dies after a large rock hits him on the head. He is the first Methodist martyr. A Calvinist, he was a friend of both Whitefield and Charles Wesley, and it was his hope to bring the two sides of Methodism back together.

After handing his ministry over to the Wesleys, Whitefield sails to America, where his preaching makes him an instant celebrity, and he works with Jonathan Edwards in igniting the religious revival known as the First Great Awakening. But he hears disquieting reports from England, where the Wesleys are preaching an Arminian rather than a Calvinist gospel. Then John preaches a sermon titled "Free Grace," in which he declares that predestination is simply contrary to Bible teaching. Attached to a printed version of the sermon is a thirty-six-stanza hymn/poem titled "Universal Redemption." It's not attributed to Charles but leaves the impression that it was written by him.

A years-long public battle ensues, through which the Wesleys and Whitefield somehow manage to stay friends. When Whitefield dies in America in 1770, physically spent at age fifty-six, John preaches his funeral service at two of Whitefield's preaching houses in London. He never mentions their theological disagreement, but he fulsomely praises God for raising up such a faithful servant as George Whitefield, who over thirty years made seven trips to America and preached at least thirty thousand times to perhaps a million or more people.

I wonder why, because of their deep friendship, they could not have worked together more closely in the Methodist Revival despite their theological disagreement. Whitefield was certainly less radical than many Calvinists of the time. He believed that not everyone he preached to was among God's elect, but he still wanted to preach the gospel to everyone because many among the elect would not know of God's grace until he told them about it. John Wesley believed that salvation was open to everyone and many would not know of God's grace until he told them about it. In both cases, they preached, and many responded positively to the news of God's grace. Perhaps despite their friendship, their large egos could not have coexisted in the same movement. It also is likely that other Calvinists, lacking a close friendship with Wesley, would not have tolerated a partnership with him. We may give God glory for them even as we lament that they never worked together as closely as they might have.

HYMNS OF RESURRECTION

Resurrection Sunday, or Easter, is the most joyful day of the Christian year. Though it specifically celebrates the resurrection of Jesus, this day has personal implications for all Christians who live in hope of resurrection life beyond this one and new birth in this one.

Charles Wesley's exuberant hymn "Christ the Lord Is Risen Today" is usually the opening hymn on Easter morning—and not just in Methodist churches. It was originally titled "Hymn for Easter Day" and was sung in public the first time in 1739 at the Foundry, a preaching house the Wesley brothers opened in a refurbished cannon factory in London. It became so popular that it was even sung in Anglican churches in Wesley's lifetime.

It's a free adaptation of a fourteenth-century hymn "Jesus Christ Is Risen Today," which first appeared in English in the 1708 hymnal *Lyra Davidica* (*Lyre of David*). It's now even sung to the same tune, thanks to the addition of "Alleluia!" at the end of each line of Charles' original hymn.[40] Variations in lyrics and the order of verses appear in different hymnals. This is a version you might be most familiar with.

Christ the Lord Is Risen Today

1. Christ the Lord is risen today, Alleluia!
Earth and heaven in chorus say, Alleluia!
Raise your joys and triumphs high, Alleluia!

40. Hawn, "Christ the Lord Is Risen Today."

Sing, ye heavens, and earth reply, Alleluia!

2. Love's redeeming work is done, Alleluia!

Fought the fight, the battle won, Alleluia!

Death in vain forbids him rise, Alleluia!

Christ has opened paradise, Alleluia!

3. Lives again our glorious King, Alleluia!

Where, O death, is now thy sting? Alleluia!

Once he died our souls to save, Alleluia!

Where's thy victory, boasting grave? Alleluia!

4. Soar we now where Christ has led, Alleluia!

Following our exalted Head, Alleluia!

Made like him, like him we rise, Alleluia!

Ours the cross, the grave, the skies, Alleluia!

Another Wesley hymn of resurrection and triumph is this exciting anthem written for Easter 1746.[41]

Rejoice, the Lord Is King

1. Rejoice, the Lord is King! Your Lord and King adore!

Mortals, give thanks and sing, and triumph evermore.

[Chorus] Lift up your heart! Lift up your voice!

Rejoice! Again I say, rejoice!

2. The Lord, the Savior, reigns, the God of truth and love.

When he had purged our stains, he took his seat above.

[Chorus]

3. His kingdom cannot fail; he rules o'er earth and heaven.

The keys of death and hell to our Jesus given.

[Chorus]

Finally, here is a hymn of praise and invitation from 1747 that clearly expresses Charles Wesley's commitment to free grace.

---

41. Hawn, "Rejoice, the Lord is King."

It was originally titled "The Great Supper" and had twenty-four verses. The United Methodist Hymnal offers two versions with different selections of verses (#339 and 616). Here is the version you are most likely to be familiar with.

Come, Sinners, to the Gospel Feast

1. Come, sinners, to the gospel feast; let every soul be Jesus' guest.

Ye need not one be left behind, for God hath bidden all mankind.

2. Sent by my Lord, on you I call; the invitation is to all;

Come, all the world! come, sinner, thou! All things in Christ are ready now.

3. Come, all ye souls by sin oppressed, ye restless wanderers after rest;

Ye poor, and maimed, and halt, and blind, in Christ a hearty welcome find.

4. My message as from God receive; ye all may come to Christ and live;

O let his love your hearts constrain, nor suffer him to die in vain.

5. See him set forth before your eyes, that precious, bleeding sacrifice!

His offered benefits embrace, and freely now be saved by grace!

SIX GOOD QUESTIONS . . . TO CONSIDER OR DISCUSS

1. If things aren't the way they're supposed to be, how are they supposed to be?

2. Have you ever kicked a bad habit or an addiction? What motivated you to change? Did you have to "hit bottom" first? Is this what Wesley meant by "poverty of spirit"?

3. Does feeling guilty motivate you to change or just make you feel bad about yourself?

4. Selena Gomez sings that the heart desires what it desires. Jeremiah 17:9 says, "The heart is devious above all else." Is this why our hearts must be renewed in God's image?

5. Does thinking of sin as a disease rather than a moral failing help you understand its hold on you?

6. Wesley says faith is more than "a train of ideas in the head." Have you ever had a faith train wreck?

Six Great Sermons, #3

"The Marks of the New Birth," Sermon 18, from 1748: These are faith, hope, and love.

4

Amazing Grace

I once served a four-month chaplaincy internship at a hospital. I gained a lot from that experience, but it felt like the longest four months of my life. In the daytime, we had a full staff of chaplains and interns, but at other times only one chaplain was on duty. Once every week or so, I had to pull the overnight shift, and it could be physically and emotionally draining.

One night, a teenage girl was brought into the emergency room. She had swallowed the contents of a big bottle of aspirin. She was hysterical, and doctors had to strap her down before sedating her and pumping out her stomach. She kept screaming, "My mama don't love me! My mama don't love me!"

While the doctors worked to save the girl, I talked to her mother. It was clear that she *did* love her daughter. But she kept calling her "my baby." And the longer we talked, the more it became clear to me that mom's attitude was a big part of their problem. This was the youngest of her several children. All the others had grown up and "gone bad," as she put it, and she didn't want that to happen to this one. So she babied the girl. Hers was a very controlling love, a conditional love, a love that demanded that the girl give up own identity to be her mama's sweet baby girl. I tried to suggest to her that her expectations might be an issue, but I don't think she understood. Whenever I think of them, I wonder how they worked it out when they got home. Did mama ever give her baby room to breathe? Did the girl ever find a constructive way to show her independence?

Theirs is a story of what I call "Love, but."

I'm sure you're familiar with it. Someone says, "You know how much I love you, but . . ." When you hear that, you know that the most important word in the sentence is not "love." The most important word is "but." This love comes with conditions. This is not genuine love, because genuine love is unconditional. To love authentically, we have to get off our buts and love without reservation.

John Wesley did not believe in "Love, but" or "Love if." He believed in "Love, period." That's the way God's love is described by Rudy Rasmus, who with his wife Juanita is pastor of a large United Methodist Church in Houston. It's love, period—end of story, no qualifications.[1] As the pop songs have it, love is all there is, and all you need is love.

Wesley likely would have preferred one of the songs written by his brother Charles, especially "Love Divine, All Loves Excelling." That's where we praise God by singing, "pure, unbounded love, thou art." Pure, unbounded love is what God shows us, and God intends that love to trigger a response of love in us. "We love because God first loved us," 1 John 4:19 says. That is, "We *can* love because God first loved us." In his *Notes Upon the New Testament*, Wesley calls this "the sum of all religion, the genuine model of Christianity."

God expresses this love through grace. Grace is God's love right here, right now; God's love yesterday, today and tomorrow; God's love always and forever; God's love without boundary or qualification—or, as Wesley might say, God's love ever-present with us in the Holy Spirit.

Let's be very clear about what grace is. Grace is gratuitous. It is not necessary. God is under no obligation to love us. God loves us simply because God's nature is loving. God acts gracefully toward us simply because God is gracious. God's love for us is totally unwarranted. We do not deserve it. We cannot earn it. That means

1. Rasmus, *Love. Period.* See also Lewis, *Fierce Love.*

that God does not pay us according to merit. God hands out gifts, not wages. If God paid according to merit, what do you think you'd get?

Grace is gratis. It's free—to us, anyway. There are no strings attached. It's on the house. It's special, but it's offered to everybody—and that makes everybody special, doesn't it?

It's a gift. The only thing you can do with it is accept it or reject it, take it or leave it. But just because it's free doesn't mean it's cheap. There is nothing cheap about grace. God pays a heavy price for it. Grace is not cheap and it's not easy. It's not easy for God—take a look at the cross—and it's not easy for us either. It's hard for us to accept something that has no strings attached. We want to earn it. We want to show that we deserve it. "Look at me, God. See how good I am! See how obedient I am! See how humble I am! It's no wonder you love me, I'm so good."

But that won't work. We cannot rely on our own uprightness. We have to rely solely on God's grace. That grace appears so unseemly, so outrageous—and yes, so wonderful and so amazing.

Are there limits to such grace? Here are two simple truths. There is nothing you can do to make God love you *more*. There is nothing you can do to make God love you *less*. Rudy Rasmus has a saying that's become popular: "God loves you, and there's nothing you can do about it!"

Preaching about grace, I often (though probably not often enough) said: "If Rudy Rasmus were here right now, he'd tell you to turn to someone and say, 'God loves you, and there's nothing you can do about it!' Then he'd tell you to turn to someone else and say, 'God loves you, and there's nothing you can do about it!'" The reaction is always warm and cheerful. Don't you feel better after hearing that God loves you without limit? Don't you feel better telling that to someone else?

Sad to say, spiritual director Henri Nouwen is probably correct when he says that "very few people know that they are loved without any conditions or limits."[2] Take it from someone who was painfully shy much of his early life, many people are afraid that

2. Nouwen, *Beloved*, 305.

they will be rejected if they reveal too much of themselves to others. We think "If they knew the real me, they wouldn't love me." We fear conditional love. We yearn for the real thing without any buts.

Accepting grace and passing it on are two keys to the life of grace. Think of it as a chain of grace. You experience grace and you pass it on. Those you love in turn love others, who—having experienced grace—love others. And so it goes. It all starts with the experience of being loved by God. You experience the love of God first through the love of others, starting—most likely—with your parents but not limited to them. And the experience changes you. It can bring you to new life in Christ.

Wesley uses the image of a house to describe how it happens. Let's call it the house of faith. Wesley says repentance is the porch, faith is the door, and inside the house is religion itself. Porch, door, interior—repentance, faith, holiness. With these three images, Wesley describes the three primary movements of God's grace that lead us to salvation. They are hardly unique to Methodism, but Wesley calls these the three pillars of Methodist doctrine—the pillars that hold up the Methodist house of faith.

House of faith
Three pillars of Methodism

The first movement of grace is the one that leads us to the porch. This movement goes by several names. In deep Methodist circles, it's often called "prevenient grace." That's an archaic and ungainly Methodist code word that I really don't like, and I rarely use it. (Supposedly it's a replacement for "preventing grace," which is what Wesley called it, using an even more archaic term, but I don't see much improvement.) It describes the grace that goes ahead of us, that surrounds us at all times and works to draw us closer to God.

I think it's better called "*everyday grace*," because it's available to everyone every day. Sometimes it's called "*seeking grace*" to describe how God seeks us out, wherever we try to hide. Sometimes it's called *"convincing grace,"* because God hopes to convince us that we cannot save ourselves; we cannot rely on our own strength; we must have a real relationship with God if we are to live to the fullest. (Sometimes it's also called *"common grace,"* but Calvinists put a spin on that term that renders its use questionable.)

This first movement of grace leads us to **repentance**. This is the porch of religion. As I said earlier, repentance is not, as is commonly preached and commonly believed, simply feeling sorry for yourself or sorry for your sins. Repentance is about *change*. Repentance is a turning point. It's a turning *away* from one way of living and a turning *toward* a better way of living. To put it simply, God allows, and even *encourages*, U-turns. How many? As many as it takes.

House of faith
The porch
Repentance

This second movement of grace is *"justifying grace."* This is the grace that pardons you for all your wrongdoing, forgives you for all your sins, and fills you with the confidence that you are saved.

Faith is the door you have to walk through. Faith, Wesley cautions us, is not merely an intellectual assent to the truth of the Bible or to a set of propositions about God or Christ. It's really not a head thing. It's a disposition of the heart. It is the sure trust and confidence that God has restored you to divine favor—and not because of your own merits but solely because of the merits of Christ. Wesley says faith is God's grand means of restoring the law of love in our hearts.[3]

---

3. Sermon 36, "Law Established Through Faith, Discourse 2," II.6, Works 5:464.

House of faith
The door
Faith

God justifies us, sets us right, by forgiving our sin. Sin is what separates us from God. By pardoning us, God reconciles us. We are now friends with God—and we are given the assurance and confidence that we can live as beloved children of God.

This is the New Birth, Wesley says. When we step through the door of faith, we are born anew. When we make this step into the house itself, the third movement of grace comes into play. This is "***sanctifying grace***," the grace that works to wholly change us.

House of faith
Inside
Holiness

Justifying grace produces a change of *relation*. Sanctifying grace produces a change of *nature*. Justification is what God does for us. God makes us friends. Sanctification is what God does in us. God makes us like Jesus. God makes us holy.

One thing we learn when we turn our lives around is how blasted hard it is to keep going in the right direction. In fact, we cannot do it on our own. Even after we have been set right with God, we tend to drift. We need more than a change of attitude and a change of relation. We need a change of nature, a change of heart. That's what God works in us through sanctifying grace. God works to remake us in the original image of God in which we were created, so that at the end of the process, we look just like Jesus.

The best end any of us can hope for, Wesley says, is holiness, or happiness in God. On the way to holiness, we recover both the favor and the image of God.[4] Justification is recovery of God's favor. Sanctification is recovery of God's image.

God's salvation is the ultimate makeover. God takes who we have become and remakes us into who God intended us to be in the first place. Salvation is restoration in the image of God. We were created in God's image, but we have put on many masks that distort that image. Through this process we call sanctification, God strips away those masks and restores us to God's image.

However long and difficult the process is, it's all grace—or, as Wesley puts it, "grace upon grace."[5] Everything good happens by God's grace. God created us by grace. God watches over us by grace. God seeks us by grace. God convinces us by grace. God saves us by grace. God justifies us by grace. God gives us new birth by grace. God regenerates us by grace. God sanctifies us by grace. God gives us assurance by grace. God glorifies us by grace. Everywhere you look, it's all grace.

It's all grace
Creating grace
Everyday grace
Seeking grace
Convincing grace
Justifying grace
Regenerating grace
Sanctifying grace
Assuring grace
Glorifying grace

---

4. Sermon 6, "Righteousness of Faith," II.9, Works 5:74.

5. Sermon 1, "Salvation by Faith," 3, Works 5:8; Sermon 34, "Original, Nature, Property, and Use of the Law," IV.4, Works 5:444

ON TO PERFECTION

Wesleyan holiness scholar Mildred Bangs Wynkoop calls John Wesley the modern-day "Apostle of Love" because he equates holiness with love.[6] True religion, he says, is having the love of God and neighbor filling your heart and governing your life, directing all your thoughts, words, and actions. "The sure effect of this is the uniform practice of justice, mercy, and truth."[7] Commenting on Matt 6:33, "Seek first the kingdom of God and his righteousness," Wesley says: "Righteousness is the fruit of God's reigning in the heart. And what is righteousness, but love?—the love of God and of all mankind, flowing from faith in Jesus Christ."[8] God's kingdom, righteousness, holiness and love are all part of a package. We live in God's kingdom when we are righteous, when we are rightly related to God and neighbor, when we live in holiness and love.

The role of faith is to lead us back to the love that we lost because of sin, Wesley says—and stirring love in us is the sole purpose of all God's commandments.[9] "Love is the sum of Christian sanctification," he says.[10] "It prepares us for and constitutes heaven."[11]

Just as love is the governing affection of God, love is our governing affection when we have the mind of Christ. Self-love and neighbor-love go together because genuine love of self that is rooted in God's love can find expression only in the love of others.[12] Still, we cannot do what we know we ought to do without the power to do it—and that power comes to us only through the Holy Spirit by God's grace.

6. Wynkoop, *Theology of Love*, 10.

7. Sermon 84, "Important Question," III.2, Works 6:498; Sermon 102, "Of Former Times," 11, Works 7:162.

8. Sermon 29, Sermon on Mount 9, 20, Works 5:387.

9. Sermon 36, "Law Established Through Faith II," II.1, II.5–6, Works 5:462–64.

10. Sermon 83, "On Patience," 10, Works 6:488.

11. New Testament Notes ,1 Cor 13:8.

12. "Letter to the Rev. Dr. Conyers Middleton," VI.6, Works: 10:68.

Wesley agrees with Calvinists and others who say that human will is free "by nature" only to do evil, but he says God has left no one "in a state of mere nature" because "every man has a measure of free-will restored to him by grace."[13] God's grace is always working in the human heart. So if you fall into sin, it's not because you lack grace but because you don't use the grace you have. If you don't think you have enough faith, "Stir up the spark of grace which is now in you, and God will give you more grace."[14]

Wesley extends the work of the Holy Spirit and God's grace beyond the confines of the Christian faith—not only "to such as have the distinct knowledge of his death and sufferings, but even unto those who are inevitably excluded from this knowledge. Even these may be partakers of the benefit of his death, though ignorant of the history, if they suffer his grace to take place in their hearts, so as of wicked men to become holy."[15]

A caution: Grace for all does not mean salvation for all. Despite its title, that hymn "Universal Redemption" allows that some people may spurn God's love and never be saved. And Wesley expects the benefits of God's grace to be fully felt only by those who know Christ. For one thing, non-Christians can never receive the personal assurance that Wesley himself received only at his Aldersgate awakening. That assurance comes through the Holy Spirit's direct testimony to a person. Wesley describes it this way: "The testimony of the Spirit is an inward impression on the soul, whereby the Spirit of God directly witnesses to my spirit that I am a child of God, that Jesus Christ hath loved me and given himself for me and that all my sins are blotted out, and I, even I, am reconciled to God."[16]

How is this "inward impression on the soul" expressed and felt? One way is through what Wesley calls "spiritual

13. "Some Remarks on Mr. Hill's Review," 64, Works 10::392.

14. Sermon 85, "On Working Out Our Own Salvation," III.4, Works 6:512–13.

15. "Letter to a Person Lately Joined With the People Called Quakers," 6, Works 10:178–79.

16. Sermon 10, "Witness of the Spirit 1," 1.7, Works 5:115.

respiration"—God's grace continually being breathed in and out, moment by moment, day by day, from now to eternity. "Grace is descending into his heart; and prayer and praise ascending to heaven: And by this intercourse between God and man, this fellowship with the Father and the Son, as by a kind of spiritual respiration, the life of God in the soul is sustained; and the child of God grows up, till he comes to the 'full measure of the stature of Christ.'"[17] This is "the life of God in the soul of a believer," the "continual inspiration of God's Holy Spirit," and the "unceasing presence of God."[18]

It's an exceptional concept with great biblical precedent. Both Hebrew and Greek use the same word for "breath" and "spirit." So consider for a moment: How long can you hold your spiritual breath? How long can you go without breathing God in and breathing God out to others? If you want to stay in relationship with God, you've got to keep breathing!

So breathe in deeply and exhale fully. Breathe in the breath of God. Breathe out praise and prayer, offering up all the thoughts of your heart. Breathe in the Holy Spirit that animates life eternal. Breathe out prayer, offering up all the words of your tongue. Breathe in the unceasing presence of our loving and pardoning God. Breathe out love in all the works of your hands. Breathe in Father, Son, and Holy Spirit. Breathe out thanksgiving with all your body, soul, and spirit. This is how you pray without ceasing. This is how you worship in spirit and truth. By this form of worship you make yourself a holy sacrifice acceptable to God. You are becoming a living stone in a spiritual house that will stand through the storms of time.

"This [is] the religion we long to see established in the world," Wesley says—"a religion of love and joy and peace, having its seat in the heart, in the inmost soul, but ever showing itself by its fruits,

17. Sermon 45, "New Birth," II. 4, Works 6:71.

18. Sermon 19, "Great Privilege of Those That Are Born of God," I.8, Works 5:232.

continually springing forth . . . spreading virtue and happiness all around it."[19]

Recovery of holiness and happiness found through intimacy with God is "the one thing needful" for every human.[20] All humans were created in the image of God. One thing this means is that *sin* is not original to our nature. *Holiness* is. Humans were "created in the image of God and designed to know, to love, and enjoy our Creator to all eternity."[21] Sin distorts that image in us, leaving us "enslaved to a depraved understanding and a corrupted will."[22] But the image is still there, waiting to be reawakened. It's as if the instrument of our lives has gone out of tune, Wesley says. We need to be retuned.[23]

The first movement of grace leads us to repentance, the porch of religion. Faith opens the door for us. The moment we give ourselves to Christ, our sins are forgiven, "blotted out," Wesley says.[24] We are pardoned of all wrongdoing, and we are justified—that is, restored to right relationship with God. We also experience New Birth, which Wesley calls the "gate" to full salvation, also known as sanctification.

"Justification implies only a relative, the New Birth a real, change," Wesley says. "The one restores us to the favor, the other to the image, of God."[25] As important as justification is, it's only the beginning. It's just the start of the change that God wants to work in us. Though we are pardoned for past sins, we are still capable of sinning. Sin no longer reigns in our lives, but it does remain—and

19. "Earnest Appeal of Men to Reason and Religion," 4, Works 8:3–4.

20. Sermon 146, "One Thing Needful," I.5; Outler and Heitzenrater, *Sermons*, 36.

21. Sermon 56, "God's Approbation of His Works," I.14, Works 6:213.

22. Sermon 141, "Image of God," II.5, II.1; Outler and Heitzenrater, *Sermons*, 17.

23. Sermon 141, "Image of God," II.5, II.1; Outler and Heitzenrater, *Sermons*, 17.

24. Sermon 19, "Great Privilege of Those That Are Born of God," 1, Works 5: 22.

25. Sermon 19, "Great Privilege of Those That Are Born of God," 1.2, Works 5: 22

so must repentance and faith.[26] "Only let it be remembered, that the heart, even of a believer, is not wholly purified when he is justified. Sin is then overcome, but it is not rooted out; it is conquered, but not destroyed."[27]

Destroying the power of sin in us is the role of sanctification. Wesley explains it simply this way: "A child is born of a woman in a moment, or at least in a very short time: Afterward he gradually and slowly grows, till he attains to the stature of a man. In like manner, a child is born of God in a short time, if not in a moment. But it is by slow degrees that he afterward grows up to the measure of the full stature of Christ."[28]

Salvation, growth into sanctification, is thus a lifelong process. It's "the entire work of God, from the first dawning of grace in the soul, till it is consummated in glory."[29] It is not only a thing of the past, dating to the moment of New Birth. "It is a present thing; a blessing which, through the free mercy of God, ye are now in possession of."[30] It also is a future hope at the end of the process, aided by grace all the way.

The end is holiness, or Christian perfection. On its face, the idea seems preposterous. Given the power of sin and the vagaries of the human heart, how can anyone seriously speak of human perfection? Wesley struggles to articulate a vision of perfection that is clear enough to satisfy his critics, and it becomes a controversy almost as big as quietism and Calvinism. "No one can be perfect!" his critics jibe. They ignore Jesus' command in Matt 5:48, "Be perfect as your heavenly Father is perfect." Given the context, it seems obvious that Jesus is thinking of perfection in love—and so is Wesley. He sees perfection as a dynamic rather than a static thing—a state of continuous growth in relationship with God rather than a finished state of being. In his best moments, he describes

---

26. Sermon 14, 1, "Repentance of Believers," 1, Works 5:156.

27. Sermon 123, "Deceitfulness of the Human Heart," II.5, Works 7:341.

28. Sermon 45, "New Birth," IV.3 Works 6:75.

29. Sermon 43, "Scripture Way of Salvation," I.1, Works 6: 44.

30. Sermon 43, "Scripture Way of Salvation," I.1, Works 6: 44.

it simply as love. "This is the sum of Christian perfection," he says. And it has two branches: love of God and love of neighbor.[31]

"Sinless perfection" it is not. Wesley insists that perfection does not imply, as some imagine, "an exemption either from ignorance, or mistake, or infirmities, or temptations. Indeed, it is only another term for holiness. They are two names for the same thing."[32]

Oswald Chambers is the author of *My Utmost for His Highest*, perhaps the most famous of all modern Christian devotionals. Chambers is a Calvinist, but he fully understands what's going on here. He says: "Christian perfection is not, and never can be, human perfection. Christian perfection is the perfection of a relationship with God."[33]

In most Methodist churches, every person who is ordained for ministry must answer these three questions:

1. Are you going on to perfection?

2. Do you expect to be made perfect in love in this life?

3. Are you earnestly striving after it?

The only acceptable response is: "Yes, by the grace of God."

Alas, the only time most laypeople hear about perfection is the Annual Conference, where Methodist pastors are questioned and then ordained. Wesley considers perfection "the grand depositum which God has lodged with the people called Methodists" and the chief reason God "raised us up."[34] But it's not likely to be a favorite topic among most Methodist preachers. It is easy to equate perfection with full sanctification and spiritual maturity, but it's hard to say much beyond that. On All Saints Sunday, you can point to many people you consider saints, but can you say they've reached *perfection* in love? It is one thing to be moving toward perfection and earnestly striving for it but another thing to expect to be made

31. Sermon 76 "On Perfection," I.4, Works 6:413.

32. Sermon 40, "Christian Perfection," 9, Works 6:5

33. Chambers, *My Utmost*, 251.

34. Sept 15, 1790 letter to Robert C. Blackbenbury; Works 13:9.

perfect in love in this life. In fact, Wesley never claims that he has reached perfection and eventually concludes that for many people, complete sanctification will come only near the moment of death, when we finally give up any pretense of ability to rescue ourselves.

SIGNS OF GRACE

God's grace comes to us in many ways. Although I was not brought up in the church, I can't remember any time I didn't know Jesus. Credit my loving parents and a babysitter my brother and I called Cam. Because I can't remember being converted, I have no conversion story to share. But I do have a *baptism* story. I was about eleven when I made my confession of faith before a board of church elders—grey men in grey suits. I have no memory of what I said, though I suspect it was what they expected and hoped to hear: "I asked Jesus into my heart by saying the sinner's prayer." Then the pastor and catechumens waded into the baptismal tank at the front of the church.

My baptism was not so much a spiritual experience as a near drowning experience. The pastor and I must have gotten our signals crossed because I was still inhaling when he pushed me under the water. I felt like I was down a long time, and I came up gagging and coughing. With many years of hindsight, I see this moment as a sign from God. Being baptized empowered me to ask questions, and I was soon taught that church was the last place you should ever question anything.

In college, I suffered what the novelist Dan Wakefield calls "your standard deconversion experience." I discovered that the faith of my childhood was not strong enough to withstand the challenges of the secular world. Or to put it another way: I discovered that my church never taught the liberating gospel of Jesus Christ. What it taught, in the name of Jesus, was shallow religious platitudes. Let me testify that once you have heard the real gospel of Jesus Christ, religious platitudes are a stomach-turning alternative.

A long string of "chance" encounters with the right people, one leading to another, kept me in love with Jesus until Linda introduced me to Methodism. Her grandfather was a Methodist minister, first in his native Ireland, then in America. In Methodism, as Ps 16:6 says, I found that the spiritual boundary lines fell in all the right places. Linda and I were married in Christ United Methodist Church in Decatur, Illinois, by a pastor named Bill Laughlin, who had gone to high school with my parents but hadn't seen them in more than twenty years. We included a confession of faith in the ceremony. Naively, we thought that was normal.

A few years later, we moved to northern lower Michigan, to the resort town of Traverse City, and became involved in the big downtown church, Central United Methodist. In the summers, we attended early morning worship on the beach of Grand Traverse Bay. Bring your own lawn chair, and don't forget the sunscreen! Out in the open, in the fresh air, with the gulls joining in the singing of God's praise—this is the way worship ought to be!

After our first daughter was born, we concluded that we were entirely too far away from grandparents, so it was time to move closer to our homes. Kansas City was about halfway between my parents in Illinois and hers in Kansas, so I found work as a copy editor at *The Kansas City Star*.

We were still unpacking in our little rental house one afternoon when a young couple came by to welcome us to the neighborhood. Before they left, they invited us to their church. Surprise!—it was another Central United Methodist. (It has a new name now: Church of the Resurrection Brookside.) We soon became involved in a lively new Sunday School class called the Mariners. There we found a vibrant faith that connected our heads and hearts in ways they had never been connected before and left us feeling, perhaps if for the first time, whole.

After a few years and the birth of another daughter, it was time to move again, this time west across the state line, into the Kansas suburbs, and eventually to a church closer to our new home. Roeland Park UMC has now, sadly, closed because of declining membership. But then was a thriving, open, accepting, and nurturing congregation. There I felt safe to seek answers to a new yearning that I was feeling, a gnawing that wouldn't go away. I felt like the car crash concussion had knocked some sense into me, but I couldn't see the bigger picture. I knew God was calling me to something beyond myself, but I didn't know what it was.

I was starting to think that my future had little to do with newspaper work. Like most journalists, I suspect, I had gotten into the field to change the world—if not in a big way, at least to make it a better place somehow. In journalism school I was taught that if you give people the facts, they will make the right decisions. It didn't take long for the real world to reveal that notion as mostly fantasy. Give people facts, and they may applaud you or hate you. Either way, they will do what they want in pursuit of what they see as their own interest. Nobody votes for the "common good." Everybody votes for "what's best for me." Few people imagine that the gospel of Jesus Christ has anything to do with it.

I got involved in the Lay Speaker program, which puts committed laypeople to work leading key ministries. I found it enriching and empowering. But Sally Haynes, a wise friend who was training for the pastorate, warned me: "It won't be enough, you know." I really *wanted* it to be enough. I was happy being an active layperson. I had drunk deeply of the lay empowerment message promoted by Episcopal lay preacher Verna Dozier,[35] and I had happily served in many lay leadership roles. I didn't want to change. I wasn't aware then of a simple truth stated by David Lowes Watson: "There is only a hair's breadth between the call to strong lay leadership in the church and the call to full time ministry."[36]

My pastor, Wally Proctor, was patient with me. One evening, after a long conversation, he gently put into words what others say they'd been aching to tell me for a long time. He said, "I think you ought to consider going into ordained ministry." I laughed it off. I had never really entertained such a thought. Happily, Wally was not offended by my reaction. Pray about it, he said. So I did. Once the idea was planted in my head, it seemed so absolutely right that I never doubted that this was precisely what God was calling me to do. Within weeks, I entered the clergy candidacy process and

35. Dozier, *Authority of the Laity.*
36. Watson, *Class Leaders,* 49.

was admitted to Saint Paul School of Theology in Kansas City. There I found my faith and understanding challenged, expanded, strengthened, affirmed. Every day, I realized more and more that this was something I was meant to do, something I was meant to be.

Looking back, it all makes sense to me. I can see how God was quietly preparing me for each step of the journey, and especially how God was molding me through key experiences and encounters with special people. Among those were several clergy: Dr. Elbert Cole, longtime pastor of Central UMC in Kansas City; retired Bishop Eugene Frank, who was "bishop in residence" at Central; and an enthusiastic young associate pastor named Adam Hamilton, who is now the lead pastor of the United Methodist Church of the Resurrection in Leawood, Kansas, the largest United Methodist church in the country. At St. Paul, my three greatest influencers were Hal Knight, professor of evangelism and all things Wesleyan; Tex Sample, professor of church and society; and Warren Carter, professor of New Testament.

These are extraordinary people. I could name dozens more, lay as well as clergy, so many names and faces of those who followed Jesus from the pews and the trenches of daily life. But when you follow Jesus, encountering extraordinary people is so common an experience that it's almost ordinary. What makes these people extraordinary is the glow of the Holy Spirit living in them. "It's in Christ that we find out who we are and what we are living for," the apostle Paul tells us. It's in Christ that I discovered who I am and what I am living for. As Paul says, it was a sheer gift, a real surprise, God handling all the details (Eph 1:11, 3:7, The Message).

HYMNS OF LOVE

"Love Divine, All Loves Excelling" is widely considered to be Charles Wesley's greatest hymn. Composed in 1747, it states the essence of Wesleyan love theology in compelling ways.[37]

37. "History of Hymns: 'Love Divine, All Loves Excelling.'"

Long popular in Britain, it has the distinction of being chosen by royalty for two recent major events: the wedding of Prince William and Kate Middleton in 2011 and the funeral of Queen Elizabeth II in 2022. However, following Anglican practice, both occasions omitted verse 2, calling on the power of the Holy Spirit. If it is not excised, verse 2 is often wildly bowdlerized. Today's so-called "evangelicals" may be enraged at the prospect of a single word in a Chris Tomlin song being changed, but Reformed folk seem to find great joy in cutting divine love down to human size.

First, there's the line "let us find that second rest." Charles probably means sanctification, justification being the unmentioned "first rest." But "second rest" sounds an awful lot like the "second blessing" of Pentecostals and other modern "enthusiasts" in the Wesleyan camp, and we can't have any of *that*, can we? It's "promised rest" in some hymnals.

The original also asks the Spirit to "take away the love of sinning." John Wesley thought it would better read "bent of sinning." Some later hymnals changed that to "our bent to sinning," which seems closer to the mark. There is some theological chatter over the difference between "love of sinning" and "bent to sinning." I think it's mostly sophistry.

In the fourth verse, Charles wrote, "Pure and sinless let us be." To avoid any association with the notion of "sinless perfection," John changed that to "Pure and spotless." Others prefer "Pure and holy." There are some other nits you might pick as well, but let's move on.

Love Divine, All Loves Excelling

1. *Love divine, all loves excelling, joy of heaven, to earth come down,*
fix in us thy humble dwelling, all thy faithful mercies crown.
Jesus, thou art all compassion, pure, unbounded love thou art.
Visit us with thy salvation; enter every trembling heart.
2. *Breathe, O breathe thy loving Spirit into every troubled breast.*
Let us all in thee inherit, let us find that second rest.

*Take away the love of sinning; (our bent to sinning); Alpha and
    Omega be.*
End of faith, as its beginning, set our hearts at liberty.
3. Come, Almighty, to deliver, let us all thy life receive.
Suddenly return, and never, never more thy temples leave.
Thee we would be always blessing, serve thee as thy hosts above,
pray, and praise thee without ceasing, glory in thy perfect love.
4. Finish, then, thy new creation; pure and spotless let us be.
Let us see thy great salvation perfectly restored in thee.
Changed from glory into glory, till in heaven we take our place,
till we cast our crowns before thee, lost in wonder, love and praise.

Another great Wesley hymn about God's love is "Jesus, Thine All-Victorious Love," from 1740. It originally had twelve verses and took its title from its first line, "My God! I know, I feel thee mine."

Later versions range from four to eight verses. Sadly, the final verse is rarely sung today.[38] I've made it verse 5 here, adding it to the four verses commonly sung today.

Jesus, Thine All-Victorious Love

1. Jesus, thine all-victorious love shed in my heart abroad;
then shall my feet no longer rove, rooted and fixed in God.
2. O that in me the sacred fire might now begin to glow;
burn up the dross of base desire and make the mountains flow!
3. O that it now from heaven might fall and all my sins consume!
Come, Holy Ghost, for thee I call, Spirit of burning, come!
4. Refining fire, go through my heart, illuminate my soul;
scatter thy life through every part and sanctify the whole.
5. My steadfast soul from falling free shall then no longer move;
but Christ be all the world to me, and all my heart be love.

---

38. "History of Hymns: 'Love Divine.'"

SIX GOOD QUESTIONS . . . TO CONSIDER OR DISCUSS

1. Do you believe in "love, but" or "love, period," or maybe both?

2. Wesley describes the house of faith as porch, door and interior—repentance, faith, and holiness. Are you in or out?

3. Have you tried spiritual respiration as a spiritual discipline? Does it "work" for you?

4. How is love the sum of Christian perfection?

5. Are you going on to perfection?

6. Can you trace the movements of God's grace in your life?

Six Great Sermons, #4

"The Scripture Way of Salvation," Sermon 43, from 1765: Wesley packs much of his theology into one sermon.

5

Growing in Grace

John Wesley always insists that he will never leave the Church of England—and he never does. But separation of his movement from the church is probably inevitable from the start. In the summer of 1739, shortly after he starts outdoor preaching, he is summoned before the Bishop of London, Joseph Butler, who orders him to quit doing it. Wesley is defiant. He declares that his Oxford fellowship assigns him to no specific diocese and therefore gives him authority to preach anywhere. "I look upon all the world as my parish," he says. "I judge it meet, right and my bounded duty to declare, unto all that are willing to hear, the glad tidings of salvation. This is the work which I know God has called me to, and sure I am that his blessing attends it."[1]

The church won't recognize what he is doing as legitimate, so Wesley creates a discipleship system that runs roughly parallel to the Anglican system but also goes beyond it. For example, he forms a "connexion" of local societies that meet during the week so that members can worship in churches on Sunday. The system works, more or less, though some Methodists are excluded from Anglican services and, in 1768, an Oxford college expels six students (Calvinists all) because they are Methodist.

---

1. Journal June 11, 1739, Works 1:201–2.

Instead of churches, he builds "preaching houses" for worship. These buildings become settings for all sorts of ministry to people in need. How does he pay for all this? In 1742, he divides society members into smaller groups called classes. The plan is to have the class leader collect one penny a week from each class member who is able to pay. Visiting everyone proves too much for the class leaders, so Wesley simply has the whole class meet for an hour once a week, focusing their time on how they are growing in discipleship. It turns out to be a brilliant solution to several temporal as well as spiritual problems, and Wesley marvels (as he often does when he has "discovered" something): This must be the way it worked in the early church, too![2]

John and Charles aren't able to be everywhere all at once, so they raise a stable of lay preachers, few of whom have advanced formal education. These are "extraordinary messengers" who have responded to "extraordinary calls" from God. Starting in 1744, John and his preachers (whom he variously identifies as his "helpers," "assistants" or "sons of the gospel") meet in conference once a year to discuss doctrine and strategy. By 1790 they are preaching in 114 circuits throughout the land.

Starting with Sarah Crosby in 1761, women also are preaching throughout the land, with Wesley's full endorsement. Mary Bosanquet Fletcher, Hannah Harrison, Eliza Bennis and Sarah Mallet are among the prominent female figures of the movement. How "extraordinary" are these messengers? Crosby records that in 1777 alone she travels 960 miles, preaches 220 times and presides over six hundred small groups. Though women preach everywhere, Wesley never appoints them to preaching circuits, because that might push the movement too close to breaking with the Church of England, which doesn't recognize women in any teaching capacity.

Despite such tact on Wesley's part, tension continues to grow between the revival and the church establishment. As an Oxford fellow, Wesley is obliged to preach there every few years. Several of his Oxford sermons are simply dynamite: the first, "Salvation

2. "The People Called Methodists," Works 8:250.

by Faith," comes barely four weeks after his Aldersgate experience. It proclaims God's grace as the source and human faith the sole condition of salvation. "The Almost Christian" in 1741 contrasts real and counterfeit followers of Christ. "Scriptural Christianity" in 1744 carries that contrast to the doors of Oxford itself. It's the last time he is allowed to preach there. "Be it so," he reflects. "I am now clear of the blood of these men. I have fully delivered my own soul."[3]

The Revolutionary War in America triggers the biggest breach. Methodist societies have been meeting in America since about 1764, led by such lay people as Robert & Elizabeth Strawbridge, Philip Embury, Barbara Heck, and Capt. Thomas Webb. In 1768, Thomas Taylor writes to Wesley requesting more preachers. Over the next few years he sends several, including Francis Asbury, who will become the face of Methodism in America for many years.

When the colonies win their independence and the Church of England goes home, American Methodists have no one to serve them communion. Wesley can't persuade an Anglican bishop to ordain a Methodist preacher, so in 1784 he does it himself. He ordains two men as deacons and consecrates Thomas Coke as a superintendent (the equivalent of bishop). At the "Christmas Conference" of 1784 in Baltimore, the Methodist Episcopal Church is born, and Coke ordains Asbury as another superintendent.

Charles Wesley, who has grown increasingly uneasy with his brother's innovations, is aghast. Church authorities think he's gone apostate. They see Wesley's action as clearly outside boundaries of proper behavior. But Wesley believes that priests are essentially the same order of ministry as bishops, so he has as much authority as anyone to ordain someone. In his mind, it's not much different than preaching without notes or praying extemporaneously. He sees the Church of England as "the most scriptural national church in the world,"[4] but "in cases of necessity I will vary from it."[5] Preaching

3. Journal Aug. 21, 1744, Works 1:470
4. "Farther Thoughts on Separation from the Church," 1, Works 13:272.
5. Sermon 115, "Ministerial Office," 16, Works 7:279.

the gospel is always his priority. If the Church of England will not claim ecclesial authority over Methodists in America, he will.

ALWAYS GROWING

Wesley sees Methodism as a restoration of early Christian practice. It's "plain, old, Bible Christianity," he says, the same "scriptural Christianity" that was practiced in the primitive church.

As such, it is a way of life. Following Jesus is not just one small facet of your many-faceted life. It's the *whole thing*. If you don't follow Jesus in everything you do, you don't follow him at all. It's not enough to follow him in one thing or another. You have to follow him in *all things*. It's not a matter of occasional convenience. It's a full-time, lifelong commitment. It's what contemporary writer Eugene Peterson calls "a long obedience in the same direction."[6]

Wesley has struggled with this commitment much of his life. As he thunders in his sermon "The Almost Christian," it's the difference between being an "almost" Christian and an "altogether" Christian. "Almost" is good enough for some things in life, but it's not good enough for following Jesus. Being an "almost" Christian doesn't count. It's "altogether" or nothing. You're "all in" or you're not in at all.

"You were *born* for nothing else," he says. "You *live* for nothing else." You were "created in the image of God and designed to know, to love and to enjoy our creator to all eternity."[7] Your life's goal is to become the person God created you to be. You are not that person now because of sin. We reflect a poor image of our creator. Sin distorts God's image in us. Sin corrupts our nature and disrupts our relationship with God. But God is loving and gracious, so God works to restore our broken relationship and restore his image in us. This is the process we call salvation. It has two parts. The first part is justification, or restoration in relationship.

---

6. Peterson, *Long Obedience*.

7. Sermon 56, "God's Approbation of His Works," I.14, Works 6:213.

We are justified, or restored in relationship with God, as a result of Jesus' suffering on the cross. It costs God a great deal, but from our human point of view, all it takes is a decision, whether that be a formal prayer or a simple declaration of acceptance. You are pardoned at the moment you give yourself to Christ. You are made right with God. You are spiritually reborn. And that's where the story ends for some people. "I'm saved," they think. "There's nothing more I need to do." That attitude is tragically shortsighted. At this point, having been born anew, you are a spiritual newborn, an infant—someone who's incapable of feeding yourself, let alone changing your own diaper. Seriously, you're not even a rug rat Christian, let alone a toddler Christian. You have some serious growing up to do.

Growth in grace is the second part of the process of salvation. We call it sanctification. It's about the restoration of God's image in you. This part can take pretty much the rest of your life. Though you are freed from the power of sin, you are still under its influence, and the Holy Spirit has a lot of work to do in you until you are perfected in love and restored to God's likeness.

Justification is a relational change. Sanctification is a dispositional change. In justifying us, Wesley says, God does something *for* us. In sanctifying us, God does something *in* us. He *changes* us from the inside out. If you're not changed from the inside out, you're not altogether Christian, Wesley says. "Nothing short of this is Christian religion."[8]

Sanctification, or growth in grace, is something God does within us, but we need to do more than cooperate with this process. We need to actively participate. Wesley's formula is simple: "God worketh in you; therefore you *can* work . . . God worketh in you; therefore you *must* work."[9] He quotes Augustine: "He that made us without ourselves will not save us without ourselves."[10]

8. Sermon 62, "End of Christ's Coming," III.5, Works 6:276.

9. Sermon 85, "On Working Out Our Own Salvation," III.3, 7, Works 6:511, 513.

10. Sermon 85, "On Working Out Our Own Salvation," III.7, Works 6:513

Or, as the apostle Paul tells us, you have to "work out your own salvation with fear and trembling" (Phil 2:12).

We do this primarily by using the "means of grace." As the name implies, these are channels through which God conveys grace to us, means that we can use to open our hearts to God's activity in us. We're not trying to earn salvation. Rather, we are trying to work out its implications in our daily lives. You are not only saved *from* something; you also are saved *for* something. But what? God is at work in you, Paul says, enabling you both to will and to work for God's good pleasure (Phil 2:13).

Means of grace
Works of piety (love God)
Works of mercy (love people)

The means of grace are of two kinds, Wesley says: "works of piety" and "works of mercy." Jesus tells us to love God and love neighbor. Works of piety arise from love of God. They are called "instituted" means of grace, or "ordinances of God," because they have their source in Scripture or were explicitly ordained by Christ. They help us abide with God. Works of mercy arise from love of neighbor. They are called "prudential" means of grace because although they were never formally instituted, experience has shown them to be prudent, or useful, for growth in holiness.

Works of Piety

Works of piety include five spiritual disciplines and the sacraments of baptism and communion. The public **Worship** of God is central to Christian identity and the primary context of human life. Worship infuses everything we do, and especially the means of grace. **Prayer**, public or private, also is central to who we are. It is "the grand means of drawing near to God,"[11] Wesley says. "All that a Christian does, even in eating and sleeping, is prayer, when it is done in simplicity, according to the order of God, without either adding to or diminishing from it by his own choice."[12]

Works of piety
Worship
Prayer
Searching the Scriptures
Fasting and self-denial
Christian conference
Baptism
Holy communion

Prayer is "spiritual respiration." It's "the breath of our spiritual life" and how we pray without ceasing.[13] Prayer is intimate conversation with God. If you don't talk to someone, how can you say that you have a relationship with that person? However, spending quality time with God means more than presenting your latest "wish list." You need to hang out with God the way you might hang out with your best friends.

That "wish list" is important, though. It's not that we need to inform God of our needs, for God surely knows them already (Matt 6:8). Rather, Wesley says, it is to inform ourselves of how dependent we are on God. Similarly, our petitions are not to move God to act, for God is always more ready to hear than we are to pray.[14] Rather, they are to move us so that we may be willing and ready to receive the good things God has prepared for us.[15]

---

11. Letter to Miss Marsh.

12. "Plain Account of Christian Perfection," Q38 A5, Works 11:438.

13. New Testament Notes, 1 Thess 5:17.

14. Collect for Proper 22, Book of Common Prayer.

15. Sermon 26, "Sermon on the Mount VI," II.5, Works: 5:332.

Prayer is primarily *worshipful* conversation with God, but there may be times when life is hard and we want to rant against God—who surely can take our abuse with understanding and, yes, grace. Consider the psalms as one model for prayer when times are hardest.

Searching the Scriptures is another way to spend time with God, and another way God conveys grace to us. Scripture is the authoritative account of God's self-revelation to us. If you don't know what God has said to others in days before you, how can you expect to recognize the authentic voice of God in your own day? How can you even ask "WWJD—What Would Jesus Do?" if you have never taken the time to read the gospels and learn what Jesus *did*?

Wesley says Scripture is "the great means God has ordained for conveying his manifold grace" to us, and its purpose is to perfectly equip us for every good work (2 Tim 3:17).[16] In one place, he calls Scripture "the only and sufficient rule both of Christian faith and practice."[17] In another place, he calls it "the whole and sole" rule of faith and practice.[18] Such is his commitment to it sufficiency and authority.

Of Scripture he affirms: "The Spirit of God not only once inspired those who wrote it, but continually inspires, supernaturally assists, those that read it with earnest prayer."[19] So you're not reading your Bible "in the dark" but with a divine light making the text clear to you. God's Spirit is there with you to help you understand. Of course, you can't take just any idea that pops into your head as a word from the Spirit. As 1 John 4:11 says, you've got to "test the spirits" to make sure how you understand a passage is authentic. That's another reason earnest prayer is essential.

Wesley notes that although the apostles and prophets were divinely inspired, sometimes they did not write from a "particular

---

16. Sermon 16, "Means of Grace," III.8, *Works* 5:193.

17. "Character of a Methodist," 1, *Works* 8.340.

18. Sermon 106, "On Faith," I.8, *Works* 7:198.

19. *New Testament Notes,* 2 Timothy 3:16.

revelation" but from the "divine light" within them.[20] They wrote not by dictation but rather a collaboration with God that left them free to speak in their own voice.[21]

Because the Bible was recorded and transmitted by humans, it has to be carefully interpreted so that we don't mistake historical and cultural norms for divine intent for everyone for all time. Where Christians differ most of the time is not over the *words* of the Bible but the *meaning* of the words. Interpretations differ widely. When people claim that the Bible is infallible, ninety-nine times out of a hundred they are claiming that a certain *interpretation* of the Bible is infallible—and, don't you know, it's *their* interpretation, not yours.

In a few more pages, we'll look more closely at Wesley's approach to Scripture.

A fourth discipline is *fasting*, (abstaining from certain foods or behaviors) or other forms of self-denial. It's easy to see how reading Scripture can help train you for righteousness, but it's hard to see what fasting has to do with anything. It has always been a difficult course, and it has fallen way out of fashion these days. You may still find it helpful to keep you in spiritual shape, just as a wrestler might fast before a meet to stay within a weight class.

Fasting helps you focus on what is most important. When you give up food for a time, the gnawing in your belly makes you realize just how important food is but also puts it in perspective. As Jesus says, quoting the Hebrew Scriptures, you don't live by bread alone but by every word spoken by God (Matt 4:4; Deut 8:3). God gives you abundant life as well as bread.

Wesley wanted his people to fast every Friday. Following Anglican practice, that meant not eating, or eating very little, from sundown Thursday to mid-afternoon or sundown Friday. You can fast on any schedule you like. If you've not done it before, get advice from those who have, and check with your doctor if you have any health concerns.

---

20. New Testament Notes, 1 Cor 7:25.
21. New Testament Notes, 1 Cor 14:32.

Ages ago, when I led a youth group, the 30 Hour Famine sponsored by World Vision was part of our yearly practice.[22] It was more than an excuse for a long lock-in. It was a profound spiritual experience for all involved—from the young people who had never known hunger before, to the middle-aged advisors (and pastor) who needed reminding of the importance of self-denial.

Besides food, you also can fast from habits or behaviors that hold you back spiritually. These can range from addiction to video games or cigarettes to binge-watching TV, yelling at your kids or spouse, or just being a grouch. Ultimately, loving others is a form of fasting or self-denial, because you put the needs of others ahead of your own. When was the last time you fasted from *your* needs to help others with *theirs*? Serving in a food kitchen occasionally may seem like a minor action, but a disciplined and vital spiritual life is made up of such actions.

A fifth discipline is **Christian conference**. We can practice this weekly in formal worship services, or in other ways both formal and informal. Every summer, the annual conferences of Methodists attract thousands of people in the geographical "conferences" in which they are grouped. These large-group meetings are sometimes mind-numbingly boring and sometimes "We have so missed the point!" infuriating, but the Holy Spirit finds surprising ways to show up anyway.

Most often, Christian conference means gathering in groups of six to a dozen people to share your triumphs and struggles on the road to spiritual growth. I am not in a small group at this time, but I was for many years, and I can testify to their value. Conference in small groups was once the heart of the Wesleyan method. You can trace the decline of the Methodist church to the day Methodists abandoned that method. We rarely conference anymore. Mostly we just have meetings. And we are spiritually impoverished for it. (You know what a meeting is. It's where the nudgings of the Holy Spirit go to die a painful and prolonged death.)

Wesley championed small groups because they worked. (Consider the AA movement today.) Disciples are not made in

22. "30 Hour Famine."

large group settings but through the relationships formed in small groups. For Wesley, joining and staying in a small group was a sign of attentiveness to the practical means of grace. As a practical theologian, Wesley was chiefly interested in transforming lives, so his was "a practical divinity" for an everyday faith.

Sacraments are those means of grace instituted by Christ himself. Like most Protestants, Wesleyans recognize only two sacraments: **baptism** and **communion**. Like the Church of England, we say that only ordained ministers may preside over the sacraments, but we extend that privilege to licensed local pastors as well.

Our approach to sacraments reflects both Roman Catholic and Eastern Orthodox understandings. For example, we baptize children as well as adults, and by sprinkling and pouring as well as by immersion, because these were among the practices of the early church. And we believe that communion is more than a ritual of remembrance. With Wesley, we believe that Jesus is present in a real way in the bread and the cup, but we do not speculate about precisely *how* this may be so. His presence, through the power of the Holy Spirit, is a mystery, something beyond our understanding that we can only celebrate with thanksgiving.

Baptism, as the Book of Common Prayer declares, is the "sacrament of new birth." It celebrates the liberating act of God, not the human response to being liberated. By contrast, in some contemporary churches, the whole business of "getting saved," culminating in baptism, seems focused on the individual's decision to accept the salvation of Jesus rather than Jesus' desire to save the person. Baptism is considered a one-time means of grace. Whether someone might need to be baptized a second time for one reason or another is hugely controversial in most faith traditions and prohibited in Methodism.

Though Christians argue endlessly over how much water is needed and how it should be administered, we ought to remember that the water is only symbolic. A lot of water has a lot of symbolic value, but it's not the *water* that baptizes, nor the *person* who applies the water. The Holy Spirit is the actor here. Everyone else is an onlooker or at most a stagehand.

In many Methodist churches, communion is offered only on the first Sunday of the month. That's a huge advance over the previous practice of offering it only quarterly. *That* practice was intended to be an expedient rather than a permanent thing; traveling elders could make it to individual churches only about once a quarter.

Wesley, of course, argues for *constant* communion—not *frequent* but *constant.*

"It is the duty of every Christian to receive the Lord's Supper as often as he can," he says.[23] Why so often? "Nothing can be more plain than that the life of God in the soul does not continue, much less increase, unless we use all opportunities of communion with God and pouring our hearts before him."[24] To maintain our relationship with God, we must stay in touch with God in every way we can. Weekly communion would seem like a good place to start. I wish you well trying to start that tradition in your church!

Some churches restrict communion to members of that church or at least that denomination or faith tradition. Methodist churches generally practice "open communion." That is, all believers of any faith tradition are invited to the table—even those who have not been baptized. That's because Wesley says communion conveys to people whatever kind of grace they need, "according to their several necessities."[25] If a non-believer finds grace in holy communion, so much the better!

Some works of piety can be found in both individual and communal practices: reading and studying Scripture, for example, and sharing our faith in one-to-one relationships, in small groups and in corporate worship.

23. Sermon 101 "Duty of Constant Communion," I.1, Works 7:147.
24. Sermon 46, "Wilderness State," II.4, Works 6:81.
25. Journal, June 28, 1740, Works 1:280.

Works of Mercy

Other means of grace are called works of mercy. These are the things we do daily in loving interaction with other people. They may be acts of kindness and compassion, or working for justice for those who are oppressed. Wesley essentially reduces these to two rules: *Do no harm to anyone. Do good to everyone.*

Works of mercy
Do no harm to anyone
Do good to everyone

There's a quotation that's often attributed to Wesley. There's no evidence that he actually said it, but I'm sure he would have agreed with it.

Do all the good you can,
By all the means you can,
In all the ways you can,
In all the places you can,
At all the times you can,
To all the people you can,
As long as ever you can.

The General Rules
Do no harm
Do good
Abide with God

Together with the works of piety, these two works of mercy—"Do no harm" and "Do good"—form the General Rules of

Methodism.[26] They have been characterized as "three simple rules."[27] They may be simple, but they are far from easy to follow. To my mind, they are similar to the three rules of Mic 6:8: Do justice, love kindness, and walk humbly with God.

Our goal, in using all the means of grace, is to become transformed, not by our own effort but by opening ourselves to God's grace. Our goal in following Jesus is to allow him to live in us, to incarnate himself in us and so live in us that we may say, with Paul, "it is no longer I who live, but it is Christ who lives in me" (Gal 2:20).

Wesley describes our journey of salvation using several images of what I call the house of faith. I introduced it to you in the last chapter. Repentance is the first step. We're standing on the porch. Then we step through the door of faith. Finally, we stand in the house of faith itself.

Wesley drops the house metaphor at this point, but others have picked it up. Andy Stanley of North Point Community Church in Atlanta has spoken of three rooms in the house of faith where we explore our relationships with God and one another more deeply.[28]

House of faith
Welcome
The foyer

When you first enter the house of faith, you stand in the foyer. This is the welcome area. This is where you are made to feel comfortable. Next is the living room. It has big, cushy chairs and sofas and recliners. It's a place to relax and get to know each other better. Lastly, there's the kitchen. This is the heart of most homes. It's where people naturally congregate because it's where food and

---

26. General Rules, Works 8:269; *Book of Discipline*, 77.

27. Job, *Three Simple Rules*.

28. Mancini, *Strategy*.

drink are dispensed. This is where you can share a cup of coffee and talk over your problems. This is where you form deep and lasting relationships.

House of faith
Relax
The living room

House of faith
Enjoy
The kitchen

The house of faith has other rooms, too—lots of rooms, according to the Audio Adrenaline song "Big House." My question for you is simple: Where are you in the house of faith?

Have you felt the movement of God's seeking and convincing grace? Have you done an about-face in your life? Have you turned away from destructive behavior and turned toward the light of Christ? Do you have at least one foot on the porch? Or are you standing on the porch looking toward the door?

Do you feel God's justifying and sanctifying grace moving in your life? Do you know God's pardon? Do you feel set right with God? Do you have the assurance and confidence that you are a beloved child of God? Then welcome to the new birth! Step through the door into the house of faith.

Here you will be welcomed in the foyer. You'll be invited into the comfort of the living room. Once you get comfortable, you'll be invited into the kitchen, the heart of it all. Here you'll feel God's sanctifying grace. You'll find yourself being changed, remade, molded moment by moment and day by day so that you are becoming more and more like Jesus.

So where are you today? Are you on the porch? Are you at the door? Are you in the house? In the foyer? In the living room? In the kitchen? Wherever you are, I invite you to step deeper into the house, to more fully experience the salvation that God offers to all. Welcome to the house of faith! I know you'll like it. It was made just for you!

WESLEY ON THE BIBLE

Though Wesley calls himself "a man of one book," he reads widely. But the Bible is primary in his life. "Yea, I am a Bible-bigot," he says. "I follow it in all things, both great and small."[29] He considers the Bible "as the one and only standard of truth, and the only model of pure religion."[30]

On the one hand, he says: "If there be any mistakes in the Bible, there may as well be a thousand. If there be one falsehood in that book, it did not come from the God of truth."[31] Because "All Scripture is given by inspiration of God" (2 Tim 3:16), Wesley says "all Scripture is infallibly true."[32] On the other hand, he insists that the meaning of any passage must be "taken in connection with the context."[33] Read out of context, or recited singly as a proof text, "any passage is easily perverted."[34] Though he affirms infallibility on issues of faith and practice, he does not extend that privilege to issues of science or historical record.[35]

He prefers a literal reading of a text. "It is a stated rule in interpreting Scripture never to depart from the plain, literal sense, unless it implies an absurdity."[36] If the literal sense of texts

29. Journal, June 5, 1766, Works 3:251.

30. "Plain Account of Christian Perfection," 2, Works 11:367.

31. Journal July 24, 1776, Works 4:82.

32. Sermon 16, "Means of Grace," III.8, Works 5:193.

33. "Plain Account of Christian Perfection," Q.33. A., Works 11:429.

34. Sermon 136, "On Corrupting the Word of God," Works 7:470; Sermon 137 in Bicentennial Edition.

35. See Jones, *Use of Scripture,* 17–36.

36. Sermon 74, "Of the Church," 12, Works: 6:395.

is absurd, and apparently contrary to reason, "then we should be obliged not to interpret them according to the letter but to look out for looser meaning."[37]

This approach follows the 39 Articles of Religion of the Anglican Church. Article VI teaches that Scripture is authoritative but never calls Scripture "infallible" or "inerrant." Wesley agrees that Scripture was delivered by divine inspiration and is a rule sufficient of itself.[38] "The Scriptures are a complete rule of faith and practice, and they are clear in all necessary points."[39]

If passages appear to contradict each other, you should "illustrate the obscure by the plainer passages."[40] And you should always read with "a constant eye to the analogy of faith."[41] This is the essence of our faith that "runs through the Bible from beginning to the end in one connected chain."[42] It is a "chain of scripture truths, and their relation to each other—namely, the natural corruption of man; justification by faith; the new birth; inward and outward holiness."[43]

Wesley also works with tradition, reason and experience to interpret Scripture. In his day, Scripture, reason and tradition were already in "the Anglican Triad." To this mix, he adds personal and communal religious experience, prompting Wesley scholar Albert C. Outler to dub the result the "Wesleyan Quadrilateral." The regrettable outcome is that some people think that tradition, reason and experience are on the same level as Scripture, rather than being subordinate to it and simply helpful means of interpreting it.

At any rate, the United Methodist *Book of Discipline's* statement of Our Theological Task states it well. Truth is "revealed in

---

37. Sermon 144, "Love of God," II.5, Bicentennial Works 4:337.

38. "Popery Calmly Considered," 1.3, Works 10:141.

39. "Letter to the Rev. Dr. Conyers Middleton," 1.15, Works 10:14.

40. Journal May 12, 1738, Works 1:102.

41. "Preface" to "Explanatory Notes Upon the New Testament," Works: 14, 253.

42. Sermon 62, "End of Christ's Coming," III.5, Works 6:276.

43. Sermon 116 "Causes of the Inefficacy of Christianity," 6, Works 7:284.

scripture, illumined by tradition, vivified in personal experience, and confirmed by reason."[44]

Tradition—or at least part of it—is important to Wesley. As a High Church Anglican, he especially looks to the primitive Christian church in its "purest ages,"—that is, its first three centuries,[45] and what he considers to be the purest expression of it in his time, the Church of England.[46] In general, though, he follows the Vincentian Canon, named after a fifth-century Gallic monk named Vincent of Lérins. It holds true the faith that has been believed "everywhere, always, by all"—or, as Jude 3 puts it, "the faith delivered to the saints." Wesley affirms: "Whatever doctrine is new must be wrong; for the old religion is the only true one; and no doctrine can be right unless it is the very same 'which was from the beginning.' "[47]

Reason is important, too. "Is it not reason (assisted by the Holy Ghost) which enables us to understand what the Holy Scriptures declare concerning the being and attributes of God?"[48] In fact, the Bible teaches a "truly rational religion."[49] Though reason interprets Scripture, it can never replace revelation from God. "Reason, however cultivated and improved, cannot produce the love of God. . . It cannot produce either faith or hope, from which alone this love can flow."[50] In brief, "It is a fundamental principle with us that to renounce reason is to renounce religion, that religion and reason go hand in hand, and that all irrational religion is false religion."[51]

44. *United Methodist Book of Discipline,* 82.

45. Sermon 132, "On Laying the Foundation of New Chapel," II.3, Works 7:424.

46. "Farther Thoughts on Separation from the Church," 1, Works 13:272.

47. Sermon 13, "On Sin in Believers," 3.9, Works 5:49.

48. Sermon 70, "Case of Reason Impartially Considered," 1.6, Works 6:354.

49. "Short History of the People Called Methodists," 131, Works 13:381.

50. Sermon 70; "Case of Reason Impartially Considered," II.8, Works 6:354.

51. "Letter to Rev. Dr. William Rutherforth," I.4, Works 14:354.

It seems only reasonable, then, that people of all religions allow one another freedom to believe as they will. "We leave every man to enjoy his own opinion, and to use his own mode of worship, designing only that the love of God and his neighbor be the ruling principle in his heart and show itself in his life by a uniform practice of justice, mercy and truth."[52]

Wesley sees no conflict between the Bible's two testaments; rather, "the closest connection that can be conceived between the law and the gospel." For example, the Law commands us to love God and neighbor and to be humble, meek, and holy. We can't do those things on our own. "But we see a promise of God to give us that love, and to make us humble, meek and holy." He concludes that "every command in holy writ is a covered promise."[53] From beginning to end "the Gospel is in truth but one great promise."[54]

READING THE BIBLE

Just as Wesley recommends "constant" communion with God through the sacrament of holy communion, he also encourages daily Bible reading. In the preface to his "Explanatory Notes Upon the New Testament," he outlines this plan:

- Set apart a little time every morning and evening to study Scripture.

- Begin and end your reading with prayer that what you read may be written on your heart.

- Read all or part of one chapter of the Old and the New Testament.

- Read "with a single eye, to know the whole will of God, and a fixed resolution to do it."

- "Have a constant eye to the analogy of faith, the connection and harmony there is between those grand, fundamental

52. "Short History of the People Called Methodists," 131, Works 13:381.

53. Sermon 25, "Sermon on Mount 5," II.3, Works 5:313–14

54. Journal, June 4, 1738, Works 1:106

doctrines, Original Sin, Justification by Faith, the New Birth, Inward and Outward Holiness."

- Frequently pause to reflect on where you have done God's will and where you have not.

- Immediately praise God for where you have been enabled to do God's will and act on those areas where you have fallen short.[55]

For daily Bible readings from the Revised Common Lectionary, go to *lectionary.library.vanderbilt.edu*, provided by the Vanderbilt Divinity Library. For a Daily Bible Reading Guide from the American Bible Society, go to *americanbible.org*. For ways of integrating your prayer life with your Bible reading, check out *The Methodist Book of Daily Prayer* by Matt Miofsky.

THOSE THREE RULES

Now about those three "simple" rules: They are part of the General Rules of the United Societies, adopted by John Wesley in conference with his preachers on May 1, 1743. Yet Wesley elsewhere maintains that following those rules is not enough to qualify anyone as a real Christian.

In his Journal in 1738, he says that God does not judge holiness to be an outward thing, such as doing no harm, doing good, or using the ordinances of God. Rather, God "sees it is the life of God in the soul; the image of God fresh stamped on the heart; an entire renewal of the mind in every temper and thought, after the likeness of him that created it."[56]

The three rules are part of "the religion of the world," he says in a sermon published in 1746. One who hungers after God "wants a religion of a nobler kind, a religion higher and deeper than this."[57]

---

55. Works: 14:253.

56. Journal, Oct 14, 1738, Works 1:161.

57. Sermon 22, Sermon on Mount 2, II.4, Works 5:268.

In an essay in 1762, he says that "although none can be a real Christian without carefully abstaining from all evil, using every means of grace at every opportunity, and doing all possible good to all men, yet a man may go thus far, may do all this and be but a heathen still."[58]

Since you cannot judge by any outward thing, it is not clear how you might know whether anyone (including yourself) remains "a heathen still." Wesley's rigorous hair-splitting about who's a "real" Christian may hit a wall here. At any rate, you can accept these three rules not as an aspirational ceiling but as a floor lower than which you do not want to go.

HYMNS OF JOY

Charles Wesley wrote one great Advent hymn and one of the most popular Christmas songs ever. The Advent hymn is "Come, Thou Long-Expected Jesus." If you don't sing this in your church every year on the first Sunday of Advent, maybe you should check the pulse of your church's music director.

Come, Thou Long-Expected Jesus

1. Come, thou long-expected Jesus, born to set thy people free;
from our fears and sins release us, let us find our rest in thee.
Israel's strength and consolation, hope of all the earth thou art;
dear desire of every nation, joy of every longing heart.
2. Born thy people to deliver, born a child and yet a King,
born to reign in us forever, now thy gracious kingdom bring.
By thine own eternal spirit rule in all our hearts alone;
by thine all sufficient merit, raise us to thy glorious throne.

The Christmas song is, of course, "Hark, the Herald Angels Sing." You probably hear it at least once every year, if only during the

58. "Blow at the Root," 5, Works 10:365.

Christmas Eve candlelight service. It originally had a much different first line: "Hark, how all the welkin rings." "Welkin" was an obscure term even then. It means "heavenly choir." In his 1753 hymnal, George Whitefield changed the line to what we're familiar with today. (Good catch, George.)

It first was published in 1739 under the title "Hymn for Christmas Day." The refrain was added to make it work with the Felix Mendelssohn tune that most of us now associate with the words without thinking.

Hark, the Herald Angels Sing

1. Hark! the herald angels sing, "Glory to the new-born King;
Peace on earth and mercy mild, God and sinners reconciled!"
Joyful, all ye nations rise, join the triumph of the skies;
With angelic host proclaim, "Christ is born in Bethlehem!"
Refrain: Hark! the herald angels sing, "Glory to the new-born King!"
2. Christ, by highest heaven adored, Christ, the everlasting Lord,
late in time behold him come, offspring of the Virgin's womb:
veiled in flesh the Godhead see; hail the incarnate Deity,
pleased with us in flesh to dwell, Jesus, our Immanuel.
Hark! the herald angels sing, "Glory to the new-born King!"
3. Hail the heaven-born Prince of Peace! Hail the Sun of Righteousness!
Light and life to all he brings, risen with healing in his wings.
Mild he lays his glory by, born that we no more may die.
Born to raise us from the earth, born to give us second birth.
Hark! the herald angels sing, "Glory to the new-born King!"

SIX GOOD QUESTIONS . . . TO CONSIDER OR DISCUSS

1. Where are you in the house of faith—foyer, living room, or kitchen?

2. How does Methodism hope to restore primitive Christian practice?

3. Which of the works of piety come most naturally to you? Least naturally?

4. Does "constant" communion seem excessive to you? Does your church offer communion even "frequently"?

5. Are you comfortable with Wesley's nuanced way of reading Scripture?

6. Do you follow a daily Bible reading plan similar to what Wesley suggests?

Six Great Sermons, #5

"Justification by Faith," Sermon 5, from 1746: Faith in Christ alone is the way you can be reconciled to God.

6

Blessed Assurance

ow is it with your soul?

That's the question John Wesley asked at the start of every small group meeting that he led. It's a question that has been passed down through the Methodist tradition for more than 275 years. In many faith traditions outside the Methodist world, it has become a standard way to open any spiritual conversation.

It's a *good* question. We often glibly ask, "How are you?" or "How's it going?" And we expect a glib and cheerful reply: "I'm great! How are you?" But "How is it with your soul?" is a much sharper question. It cuts deeper and is harder to evade. Some people think it's the equivalent of "How's your spiritual life?" But it's a bigger question than that. Your "soul" is not some wispy, disembodied you. Your soul is the whole you, everything there is about you—body, mind, spirit, relationships.

So the question means, "How is it with your body, mind and spirit—and how are you getting along with others?" How are you and God? How are you and your neighbor? How are you and your boss, and your children, and your spouse, and that wacko who lives down the lane, and all the other folks in your life? And, yes, how are you getting along with yourself? Is your inner life healthy? Or do you beat yourself up all the time over failings real and imagined?

Considering the question and answering it is important. But what's more important is giving your answer to another human being who cares enough about your welfare that he or she will not let you wriggle away from the question but instead will insist that you answer fully and honestly, and then will hold you accountable for continued spiritual growth, knowing that your healthy growth in spirit also will mean healthy growth in body and mind and relationships.

Every one of us needs a small group of special friends who will love us through the hard places in our lives and keep asking, "How is it with your soul?" John Wesley insisted that Methodists become part of such a group and stay involved in it—and if they didn't, he kicked them out of the movement, at least temporarily. It's a discipline that we in the modern church are scared to even think about, if only because we have lost any sense of being a movement rather than a church.

Wesley put a lot of stock in small groups. I think we might be better off today if we did, too. He is sometimes given credit for inventing the small group, but he didn't. In fact, the more he thought about it, the more he realized that he simply rediscovered what the earliest Christian communities did in their urban house churches in Corinth and Ephesus and Thessalonica and Rome and all those other places we read about in the New Testament—and what the Moravians had discovered before him.

Wesley organized his people into three kinds of groups. The Society was the large group, similar to what we think of today as a congregation. Classes were groups of about a dozen that met weekly for sharing and support and accountability. Bands were groups of maybe half a dozen that enforced a discipline that we might describe today as "rigid."

The Society meetings were necessary for proclaiming the good news of Jesus and casting a vision for the way Jesus followers ought to live. But Wesley knew that real growth in discipleship happens primarily in face-to-face meetings in a small group. From there, it has a ripple effect. It touches you, and through you it touches others, and through them it touches still more. In this way, the world is transformed. It starts with individual change, but it cannot stop there.

Wesley sees Christian discipleship as a powerful combination of personal piety and social action—a combination that can never be separated. Following the Great Commandment of Jesus, Wesley says that our lives center on the love of God and neighbor. In fact, he says that God has so mingled our lives together that whatever grace we have received individually we are *compelled* to share with others. We just can't keep it to ourselves. That's what grace does. It just bubbles up in us and overflows to others.

Solitary religion? Just "Jesus and me"? Forget about it! Wesley says: "'Holy solitaries' is a phrase no more consistent with the gospel than 'holy adulterers.' The gospel of Christ knows of no religion but social; no holiness but social holiness. 'Faith working by love' is the length and breadth and depth and height of Christian perfection."[1]

Some people misunderstand the Methodist commitment to social action. They accuse us of trying to "earn our way to salvation." That's either a caricature or a slander, depending on how charitably you view the person making it. I have never met a Methodist who thought that earning salvation was remotely possible, let alone desirable.

We are simply trying to follow what James the apostle calls "the royal law" of loving God and neighbor (Jas 2:8). We're trying to make it a way of life. The goal of Christian living, as we see it, is to be remade in the loving image of Jesus. Yes, as Paul the apostle affirms, "the only thing that counts is faith working through love" (Gal 5:6).

Three words are important here. They are formed from the ancient Greek word "ortho," meaning "right." The first word is "orthodoxy." That means "right belief" or "right doctrine." The second word is "orthopraxy." That means "right action." Finally, there's "orthopathy." That means "right heart." Christianity in the Wesleyan tradition is a heart religion. It's love reigning in the human heart.

1. "List of Poetical Works: Preface to Hymns and Sacred Poems," Works 14:321.

Wesley says, "You know that the great end of religion is to renew our hearts in the image of God."[2]

The term "orthopathy" was coined by Wesley scholar Ted Runyon.[3] Orthopathy is the "Methodist Middle" standing between the extremes of normal orthodoxy and orthopraxy—the "extreme center," Wesley scholar Scott J. Jones calls it.[4] In Wesley's system of "practical divinity," beliefs and behavior are one. Faith and practice are linked. Personal salvation must express itself in social action. Piety must show itself in mercy. Faith must present itself in inward *and* outward ways. It adds up to holiness of heart *and* holiness of life, having the mind of Christ and the heart of Christ, being both like-minded and like-hearted, the reign of God achieved in the life of the believer.

Orthodoxy in doctrine is important, but we are not obsessed with theological purity. Wesley says there are two kinds of religious beliefs: those that are essential to salvation, about which all Christians must agree; and those that are not essential to salvation, about which Christians must be free to disagree. We are "as fixed as the sun" about the main branches of Christian doctrine, Wesley says,[5] "but as to all opinions that do not strike at the root of Christianity, we think and let think."[6]

This kind of openness has been sorely tested in the United Methodist debate over homosexuality, and we have all been found lacking. Since the outcome of this debate is schism—or at least a crackup within the denomination—the openness of some Methodists to "think and let think" has been exposed as shallow. Some of us think that our opinions about human sexuality *do* strike at the root of Christianity, so we are not willing to worship with, or be in fellowship with, those who disagree. Opinions must influence practice, of course. Questions of who can be ordained and who can be married are fundamental to our practice, and sharp differences

2. Sermon 44, "Original Sin," III.5, Works 6:64.

3. Runyon, *New Creation*, 149.

4. Jones, *Extreme Center*.

5. Sermon 39 "Catholic Spirit," III.1, Works 5:502.

6. "Character of a Methodist," 1, Works: 340.

of opinion here are unlikely to be bridged. We cannot pretend that these differences do not exist; neither should we condemn others for holding opinions different from our own.

The prospect of schism mortified Wesley. He says, "May we not be of one heart, though we are not of one opinion?"[7] He called schism "a grievous breach of the law of love."[8] On the other hand, he also said he would "be under an absolute necessity of separating from" any organization that required of him "such terms of communion as I could not in conscience comply with."[9] Both "conservatives" and "progressives" in the United Methodist debate claim this necessity in their refusal to obey "unconscionable" rules proposed or imposed by the other.

The general Methodist openness to people with whom we disagree is often misunderstood as "latitudinarianism," or indifference to truth. Nothing could be further from the truth! It is a testimony to our belief that all humans are made in God's image and deserving of respect, even (especially!) when we don't see things alike. "It is an unavoidable consequence of the present weakness and shortness of human understanding that several men will be of several minds, in religion as well as common life." Wesley says. "So it has been from the beginning of the world, and so it will be 'till the restitution of all things.'"[10]

It's all about freedom. Wesley says: "Condemn no man for not thinking as you think. Let everyone enjoy the full and free liberty of thinking for himself. Let every man use his own judgment, since every man must give an account of himself to God."[11]

He especially condemns "a narrowness of spirit, a party zeal, a being straitened in our own bowels; that miserable bigotry which makes many so unready to believe that there is any work of God but among themselves."[12]

7. Sermon 39, "Catholic Spirit," 1.4, Works 5:493.

8. Sermon 75, "On Schism," I.11, Works 6:406.

9. Sermon 75, "On Schism," 1.17, Works 6:409.

10. Sermon 39, "Catholic Spirit," I.3, Works 5:494

11. "Advice to the People Called Methodists," Works 8:357.

12. "Plain Account of the People Called Methodists," 1.2, Works 8:257.

"You can believe anything and be a Methodist," doubters scoff. In general, that might be so, but in countless specifics, it's simply untrue. Methodists may vary widely in their understanding of many things, but they are bound by certain doctrinal standards. Historically these are set down in Wesley's fifty-three "standard" sermons (similar to the homilies supplied to Anglican preachers by the likes of Thomas Cranmer, the Archbishop of Canterbury); Wesley's *Explanatory Notes Upon the New Testament*; the General Rules of the United Societies; the Articles of Religion drafted by Wesley, based on the Anglican Articles; and, in some traditions, also the Evangelical United Brethren Confession of Faith.

Two key Wesleyan doctrines are not unique to us, but we put more emphasis on them than most other faith traditions. The first is assurance of salvation. Wesley knew the value of assurance because he fretted for many years over whether he was really saved. Assurance of salvation is the "common privilege of all believers," Wesley says. He calls it "the testimony of the Spirit." It's "an inward impression on the soul, whereby the Spirit of God directly witnesses to my spirit that I am a child of God, that Jesus Christ hath loved me and given himself for me and that all my sins are blotted out, and I, even I, am reconciled to God."[13]

Assurance leads to another important notion—that of Christian perfection. In some translations, Heb 6:1 says, "Let us go on toward *perfection*." Other translations say, "Let us go on to *maturity*." That's the true sense of it. Christian perfection is Christian maturity. We cannot claim that we are free from error or without sin. We can claim that we are being perfected in love until we become just like Jesus.

When we say that we are "going on to perfection," we mean that we are being remade in the image of God and becoming the persons God created us to be. For us, "*going on* to perfection" and "*being* saved" are words for the same process. We are moving toward fullness in perfection and salvation.

Salvation, Wesley says, is "a present deliverance from sin, a restoration of the soul to its primitive health and its original purity.

13. Sermon 10, "Witness of the Spirit 1," 1.7, Works 5:115.

It's a recovery of the divine nature and the renewal of our souls after the image of God in righteousness and true holiness, in justice, mercy and truth."[14]

Here's a fair summary: *The Wesleyan Way is practicing the means of grace in community with others who seek a holy and happy life as we are all shaped in the loving image of Christ.*

GENUINE MORALITY

Sadly enough, when it comes to social action, many Christians believe in quietism. That is, they'd just as soon not get involved. John Wesley might understand that attitude, but only up to a point. He doesn't have much use for top-down political change. He believes that society should be transformed chiefly through the change in the hearts of individuals through salvation and spiritual rebirth and only secondarily through political change and revolution.

However, he has a holistic view of holiness. Social holiness is not just a pleasant byproduct of inward holiness; it's the flip side of it—as in, you can't have one without the other. Salvation is an inward change that always evidences itself in outward behavior. A good heart always shows itself in good works. Individual salvation always leads to social gospel. If it doesn't, the result is what Wesley calls "that grand pest of Christianity: a faith without works."[15] Works can never justify anyone in the eyes of God, but "if good works do not follow our faith, even all inward and outward holiness, it is plain our faith is worth nothing; we are yet in our sins."[16]

"Christianity is essentially a social religion," Wesley says. "To turn it into a solitary one is to destroy it."[17] It takes a village to raise a Christian. "Nothing can be more sure than that true Christianity cannot exist without both the inward experience and outward

---

14. "Farther Appeal to Men of Reason," I.3, Works 8:47.

15. Sermon 61, "Mystery of Iniquity," 19, Works: 6:259.

16. Sermon 35, "Law Established Through Faith," 3.6, Works 453–54.

17. Sermon 25, "Sermon on the Mount IV," 5, Works 5:29.

practice of justice, mercy, and truth; and this alone is genuine morality."[18]

You cannot grow in grace without works of piety and mercy.[19] They are inseparable.[20] Inward holiness is love of God; outward holiness is love of neighbor. If there's ever conflict between them, "works of mercy are to be preferred."[21] Since we cannot see God, we should serve God in those we *can* see—and God receives our service as if God were standing visibly before us and receiving the service in person.[22]

Thus the Methodist Revival always leans into social activism. "Be never weary of well-doing," Wesley says. "Never look back, for you know the prize and the crown are before you."[23] A couple of examples are especially noteworthy.

Use of Money

Just as Wesley offers his societies "Three Simple Rules" for living, he also has a three-point plan for how to use money. The first rule is easy to understand: "Earn all you can." Be industrious. Engage in honest labor that does not demean or harm you or another person. Work diligently and make lots of money. That sounds a lot like the good old Protestant work ethic. Anybody have an argument with that?

But there's more. The second rule is, "Save all you can." Wesley is not talking here about storing money in the bank. Christians are not to lay up treasures. "This is a flat, positive command, full as clear as 'Thou shalt not commit adultery.'"[24] No, when he says, "Save all you can," he means, "Spend as little as you can." Be frugal. Live simply. Do more with less. That is radically countercultural in

18. Sermon 125, "On Living Without God," 14, Works 7:353

19. Sermon 48, "Self-Denial," II.6, Works 6:112.

20. Sermon 92, "On Zeal," III.10, Works 7:66.

21. Sermon 92, "On Zeal," II.9, Works 7:61.

22. "Plain Account of Christian Perfection," Q.38 A.8, Works 11:440.

23. Introductory Letter to Journal, Works 1:9.

24. Sermon 28, "Sermon on Mount 8," 22, Works 5:373.

today's world where the daily mantra is, "Spend all you can." No, Wesley says. Don't spend it. Save it. Save it so you can give it away.

That's the third rule for the use of money, and it's the point of the whole thing. "Give all you can," Wesley says. Be generous. Share with others. God does not bless you with money so you can spend all of it on yourself. God blesses you with money so that you'll have more to share with others.

What proportion should you give? It's a balancing act, considering many needs.

"Render unto God, not a tenth, not a third, not half, but all that is God's, be it more or less; by employing all on yourself, your household, the household of faith, and all mankind, in such a manner that you may give a good account of your stewardship."[25] In other words, contrary to what you may think or have been told, Wesley does not say that you must impoverish yourself to be faithful to God's calling in your life, only that you must be faithful in how you use the money that comes into your hands. And if you have accumulated enough to pass some on to your children, he advises, "Leave them enough to live on, not in idleness and luxury, but by honest industry."[26]

Raised in poverty, Wesley lives frugally all his life. His publishing ventures bring in an estimated £30,000 over his lifetime, but he gives most of it away. For sixty years, no matter what his income, he lives on £28 a year. A powdered wig is a sign of professional status for clergy, but he thinks wigs are a waste of money, so he wears his hair unfashionably long. He hates signs of luxury. If you knew the realities of poverty, he says, how "could you lay out money in ornaments or superfluities?"[27]

You only imagine that people are poor because they are lazy, he says. "One great reason why the rich in general have so little sympathy for the poor is because they so seldom visit them. Hence it is that, according to the common observation, one part of the world does not know what the other suffers. Many of them do not

25. Sermon 50, "Use of Money," III.6, 135.
26. Sermon 126, "On the Danger of Increasing Riches," 17, Works 7:362.
27. Journal, Feb. 8, 1753, Works 2:280.

know because they do not care to know: they keep out of the way of knowing it and then plead their voluntary ignorance as an excuse for their hardness of heart."[28]

Slavery & Racism

Wesley is firmly against slavery and racism, the pernicious doctrine created to justify slavery. One of his last letters is to William Wilberforce, who is fighting for the abolition of slavery in Britain. In that letter he calls slavery an "execrable villainy, which is the scandal of religion, of England, and of human nature."[29]

His 1778 pamphlet titled "Thoughts Upon Slavery" is said to be as influential as the novel *Uncle Tom's Cabin* in turning minds in America against slavery. Among his thoughts:

> And no human law can deprive him of that right, which he derives from the law of nature. If therefore you have any regard to justice, (to say nothing of mercy, nor of the revealed law of God) render unto all their due. Give liberty to whom liberty is due—that is to every child of man, to every partaker of human nature. Let none serve you but by his own act and deed, by his own voluntary choice."[30]

In America, members of Methodist societies are forbidden to own slaves, and Methodist worship is open to Black and white alike. By the early 1800s, one of every four Methodists in the United States is Black. However, slave owners soon find ways to circumvent society rules, and Blacks are gradually pushed out of churches, forcing them to create their own societies and houses of worship.

The story of Richard Allen is illustrative. Born in slavery, Allen purchases his freedom and becomes an active member of St. George's Methodist Episcopal Church in Philadelphia. He's even

---

28. Sermon 98, "On Visiting the Sick," I.3, Works 7:119.
29. Letter to William Wilberforce.
30. Wesley, "Thoughts Upon Slavery."

allowed to preach—to Black church members anyway. But white members keep changing the rules of engagement. A crisis comes in the summer of 1787, the summer of the Constitutional Convention across town in Independence Hall. One Sunday morning, white ushers yank Black members out of pews to force them to sit elsewhere. Allen leads Blacks out of the church. He becomes the first Black man ordained in the Methodist Episcopal Church, and he later founds the African Methodist Episcopal Church.

You might think that now might be a good time for "mainstream" Methodism to reconcile and be reunited with the Black churches that were once forced out. But what makes you think anything would be significantly different today from what it was 250 years ago, or even more recently?

Women's Rights

Because he encourages some women to preach, it should not be surprising that Wesley also encourages equal rights for women. "By what argument do you prove that women are not naturally as free as men? And if they are, why have they not as good a right to choose their governors? Who can have any power over free, rational creatures, but by their own consent? And are they not free by nature as well as men? Are they not rational creatures?"[31]

He says the way women are commonly treated is a "barbarity," and he encourages women to resist. "Yield not to that vile bondage any longer. You, as well as men, are rational creatures. You, like them, were made in the image of God; you are equally candidates for immortality; you too are called of God, as you have time, to do good unto all men."[32]

As in America, Wesley's vision of freedom fades fast, so also in Britain. In 1803, male British Methodists ban women from preaching, though some refuse to quit.

---

31. "Some Observations on Liberty," 23, Works 11:101.
32. Sermon 98, "On Visiting the Sick," III.7, Works 7:126.

Transplanted to American soil, Methodism quickly assumes American traits. In 1784, after Americans have won their independence from England, Wesley rewrites the Anglican Book of Common Prayer and sends two thousand copies to America. Members of the new Methodist Episcopal Church willingly adopt his ideas for Sunday worship but mostly ignore the bulk of his work. They are so done with Anglican piety—and with direction from John Wesley!

Methodist circuit riders ride the crest of the wave of westward expansion. "Shouting Methodists" plant a church in every new settlement. "Organized to beat the devil," as one account has it,[33] they are for many decades the soul of the nation. As the movement morphs into a denomination, it suffers several fractures over questions of equality—Black/White, lay/clergy, male/female, rich/poor, bishop/elder. The biggest division comes in 1845, over slavery, and the church splits in two, North and South, as the nation itself will 16 years later. Those who think Methodism has gone stale follow Phoebe Palmer and others into Holiness churches: Nazarene, Wesleyan, Free Methodist, Pentecostal and—another import from England—the Salvation Army. Meantime, missionaries from America and Britain take the message around the world, making Methodism a truly global phenomenon.

How vital is this phenomenon today? As long as he is alive, Wesley holds Methodism together with his iron will. But he fears that his vision of renewed Christian community will not last. Only a few years before his death, he writes: "I am not afraid that the people called Methodists should ever cease to exist either in Europe or America. But I am afraid, lest they should only exist as a dead sect, having the form of religion without the power. And this undoubtedly will be the case, unless they hold fast both the doctrine, spirit, and discipline with which they first set out."[34]

He is thinking specifically about Methodists being corrupted by the accumulation of wealth. However, his remarks have such a gloomy "prophetic" tone that they are frequently quoted by

33. Ferguson, *Organizing to Beat the Devil*.

34. "Thoughts Upon Methodism," Arminian Magazine, 1787.

anyone with any grievance against any Methodist body, doctrine or inclination.

Has Methodism become a dead sect? I don't think so, though it is obvious that these are tough times to be Methodist. The United Methodist Church and the breakaway Global Methodist Church both struggle to find new measures of themselves. Distracted by so many things, it's hard for anybody to keep the main thing the main thing. In this time of ferment, when we all look to some form of revival, these two bodies of believers especially need the daily prayers of all who labor to keep the Wesleyan vision alive.

* * * * *

I once had a conversation with a man who did not attend worship with his wife, though he sometimes did accompany her to non-threatening "social" events at the church. He had an easy explanation for why he didn't come to worship: "I've got *issues* with the church!" I countered: "You think *you've* got issues. I *work* for the church. I've got *lots* of issues. Want to sit down sometime and talk about our issues?" He never took me up on the offer.

In more than thirty years in active ministry, and twenty years before that in lay leadership of the church, I've never let any "issues" get between me and Jesus. And I won't now. I turned to the United Methodist Church because I found it to be "a more excellent way" (1 Cor 12:31) of following Jesus than I had encountered before. I still find it to be so. This is more than "Dance with the one that brung you" sentimentality. I act out of the conviction that, despite its many faults—don't get me started!—the way of the United Methodist Church is closest to the Methodist Way and the Wesleyan Way and the Jesus Way.

John Wesley stayed in the Church of England despite his misgivings about many things because he thought it was "the most scriptural national church in the world." Similarly, I think the United Methodist Church is the most scriptural church in the world, though I readily concede that faithful believers can find a good home in other places. So I won't jump ship, no matter how many icebergs loom ahead. Kindly spare me the tired Titanic comparisons. Methodists of *all* stripes have wasted too much time rearranging deck chairs. It's time for all of us to drop our pretensions of theological superiority and simply preach the gospel of Jesus Christ. Nothing else is faithful either to the Wesleyan tradition, or to our God.

* * * * *

At the start of this book, I offered an outline of the Wesleyan way of salvation. Let me run through it briefly one more time. See if it doesn't make more sense now than it may have earlier.

> **God's love** is revealed by **grace.**
> It sparks **repentance** and inspires **faith.**
> It ignites **rebirth** and animates **holiness,**
> creating **happiness.**

It all begins with God's great love for every human being. God's love is revealed throughout our lives, grace upon grace. Even before we are aware of our need for salvation, God's everyday grace works within us to convince us to turn to God in repentance and faith. God's justifying grace reconciles us, bringing us into right relationship with God, regenerating us in spiritual rebirth. God's sanctifying grace works within us to cleanse our hearts and minds and make us just like Jesus, holy and happy, fit for God's kingdom of love and grace.

May God's grace shine upon you, leading you to be always turning toward the light of the Holy Spirit, inspiring you to greater faith, igniting rebirth in your heart and animating holiness and happiness in your life.

DISTINGUISHING MARKS

More than thirty-five years ago, a novelty book was published in the spirit of comedian Jeff Foxworthy's routine "You might be a redneck if..." The book is titled *You Might Be a United Methodist If*...[35] It's a light-hearted look at some of the peculiarities and foibles

35. Walker, *You Might Be.*

of United Methodism, such as "You might be a United Methodist . . . if you've ever sung a gender-inclusive hymn" or "if you're asked to donate money to a 'special offering' every other Sunday."

John Wesley has his own ideas about what it means to be a Methodist. In a booklet he wrote titled "The Character of a Methodist," he lists ten distinguishing marks of a Wesleyan follower of Jesus.[36] You can find more than ten if you look carefully, but see if you don't recognize yourself in these.

1. *You might be a Wesleyan* if the Holy Spirit fills your heart with the love of God.

2. *You might be a Wesleyan* if you are joyful in the Lord.

3. *You might be a Wesleyan* if you are not anxious about tomorrow.

4. *You might be a Wesleyan* if you cast all your cares on the Lord.

5. *You might be a Wesleyan* if you are pure of heart.

6. *You might be a Wesleyan* if you love others as you love yourself.

7. *You might be a Wesleyan* if you do evil to none but good to all.

8. *You might be a Wesleyan* if your chief desire is to do God's will.

9. *You might be a Wesleyan* if you always have a clear conscience toward God.

10. *You might be a Wesleyan* if you strive for God's glory in all that you do.

These, Wesley says, are the distinguishing marks of a Methodist. Why, you may object, these are nothing but the common principles of Christianity! And Wesley would say, "Yes! That's the point! We're all one in Christ!"

And yet there are some things that Wesleyans especially emphasize that other Christians do not. You might call these "the five *further* marks of a Wesleyan."

36. "Character of a Methodist," *Works* 8:339–47.

11. *You might be a Wesleyan* if you are certain that you are saved by God's grace alone, for the purpose of loving God and neighbor.

12. *You might be a Wesleyan* if you are certain that, by the grace of God, you are going on to perfection in love

13. *You might be a Wesleyan* if you believe in the unity of faith and works, or "faith working by love."

14. *You might be a Wesleyan* if you are committed to social justice, or in Matt 23:23 what Jesus called "the weightier matters of the law"—that is, justice and mercy.

15. *You might be a Wesleyan* if you know that following Jesus is not agreeing to a system of theology, far less a philosophy or ideology. It's engaging in a vibrant relationship with the living God revealed through Jesus Christ.

Wesley was once asked, "What religion do you preach? What's it good for?"

He replied: "What religion do I preach? The religion of love . . . What is this good for? To make all who receive it enjoy God and themselves, to make them, like God, lovers of all, contented in their lives and crying out at their death, in calm assurance, 'O grave where is your victory! Thanks be to God, who gives me victory, through my Lord Jesus Christ!'"[37]

And so it was that on his deathbed, John Wesley tried to sing the Isaac Watts hymn, "I'll Praise My Maker While I've Breath," and when he ran out of breath, he died.

RENEWING OUR COVENANT

The Wesley Covenant Renewal Service is widely considered one of the finest expressions of Wesleyan theology designed for use in public worship. Alas, it not widely celebrated in churches today.

Thanks to their parents, the Wesley brothers were familiar with the Puritan tradition of covenant renewal. John adapted the

37. "Earnest Appeal to Men of Reason and Religion," 19, Works 8:8.

work of seventeenth-century Puritan pastor Richard Alleine (Allen) to create a renewal service for the Methodist society in London. He recorded that 1,800 people attended the first such event on the evening of August 11, 1755.[38] He repeated the service on various dates as he traveled to various places and published the liturgy and directions for using it in 1780. By that time, it had become a New Year's tradition, accompanied by a celebration of Holy Communion and a hymn that Charles published in 1762, "Come, Let Us Use the Grace Divine."[39]

When I was a pastor, my churches commonly celebrated the service on the second or third Sunday of January, often on the same Sunday that we celebrated the Baptism of Jesus and renewed our own baptismal promises. The climax of the covenant liturgy is a prayer that is repeated by all. Here is the version we used, employing updated language:

Wesley Covenant Prayer

O Lord my God, I give myself completely to you.

I am no longer my own, but yours.

Put me to what you will. Rank me with whom you will.

Put me to doing. Put me to suffering.

Let me be employed for you or laid aside for you.

Let me be exalted for you or brought low for you.

Let me be full. Let me be empty.

Let me have all things. Let me have nothing.

I freely and heartily yield all things to your pleasure and disposal.

Now, O gracious and blessed God, Father, Son and Holy Spirit, you are mine, and I am yours.

Let this covenant made on earth continue for all eternity. So be it. Amen!

---

38. Journal, *Works* 2:339.
39. Hawn, "History of Hymns: 'Come, Let Us Use the Grace Divine.'"

May that become your frequent prayer as you continue to dedicate yourself to God and God's work in our midst.

You can find several versions of the full liturgy at several locations on the internet. The theme of complete surrender of your life to God obviously aligns with many of John Wesley's concerns, from his earliest to his last days. You can find the hymn "Come, Let Us Use the Grace Divine" in many hymnals with few changes from the original (it's #606, without music, in the United Methodist Hymnal). Its common meter works well with the tunes "Kingsfold," "Azmon," "Amazing Grace," or "Dundee."

Come, Let Us Use the Grace Divine

1. Come, let us use the grace divine, and all with one accord,
in a perpetual covenant join ourselves to Christ the Lord;
Give up ourselves, through Jesus' power, his name to glorify;
and promise, in this sacred hour, for God to live and die.
2. The covenant we this moment make be ever kept in mind;
we will no more our God forsake, or cast these words behind.
We never will throw off the fear of God who hears our vow;
and if thou art well pleased to hear, come down and meet us now.
3. Thee, Father, Son, and Holy Ghost, let all our hearts receive,
present with thy celestial host the peaceful answer give;
to each covenant the blood apply which takes our sins away,
and register our names on high and keep us to that day!

A sung version of the "Covenant Prayer" can be found in #3115 of the green *Worship & Song* United Methodist hymnal supplement. The Worship Collective of United Methodist Church of the Resurrection in Leawood, Kansas, also offers the worship song "I Am Yours." Find it on the Collective website (*https://collective.cor.org/songs-for-worship-1*) or on YouTube (*https://www.youtube.com/watch?v=vEIQu8c428E*).

Magrey R. deVega writes about the covenant service in *One Faithful Promise*, but the service itself is included only in accompanying guidebooks. The service is also at the end of *Almost Christian: A Wesleyan Advent Experience*. (All are published by Abingdon Press, Nashville, 2016.)

SIX GOOD QUESTIONS . . . TO CONSIDER OR DISCUSS

1. How is it with your soul? Remember, your soul is the whole you, physical as well as spiritual, mental as well as relational.

2. Are you part of a small group where you can just "be yourself" with others?

3. What are the differences between orthodoxy, orthopraxy, and orthopathy?

4. Do you have to always agree with others to love them or work with them?

5. If salvation doesn't show itself in your behavior, are you really saved?

6. If all humans are created in God's image, how can anyone be racist or sexist or any other "ist"?

Six Great Sermons, #6

"The Circumcision of the Heart," 17, from 1733: Love is the sum of God's perfect law.

Appendix 1

Small Group Tutorial

John Wesley organized his people into societies, classes and bands to help them grow in grace. Here is a brief guide to small group ministry patterned after these early Methodist classes. These groups help build strong disciples by putting the "method" back into Methodism. I call them Life Groups, but feel free to call them Wesleyan Classes or Growth Groups or whatever you think best describes their purpose.

Five Ws of Life Groups

Who—Seven to twelve people
What—meet together
When—for about one hour every week
Where—usually at someone's home
Why—to build stronger relationships with God and one another.

A group can meet anytime and anywhere its members agree on. Homes are an ideal setting, but groups also can meet in a church building or another public venue—even a restaurant or coffee shop if the setting works.

Weekly meetings are best for most groups. Any longer gap between meetings can defeat the purpose of the group. Try to keep each meeting to one hour. Groups typically have no formal leader but share or rotate leadership and hosting roles.

The meeting focuses on holding group members accountable for growth in discipleship and Christian formation. Here's one format:

- 10–15 minutes—gathering, informal conversation, refreshments, prayer
- 35–40 minutes—accountability and sharing.
- 10 minutes—prayer, dismissal, upcoming plans if different than normal

A group member could read a short passage of Scripture or share a brief devotional right before the opening prayer. However, this is not a study group, so don't make it into one.

You can occasionally "break format" and do something different—say, a meal or recreational activity, possibly including guests, for "team building" or for expansion.

The group can stay together for as long as members desire to meet. To avoid the temptation to turn inward and become cliquish, the group must be able to successfully integrate newcomers. Newcomers can join a group by invitation from a group member and agreement by the others. You don't all need to be from the same church. In fact, because of the group's nature, it ought to be open to anyone.

If more than seven people regularly attend, you can break up into groups of three or four for sharing, then come back together for the closing. That way, everyone has plenty of time to speak. If you often break up into smaller groups, make sure the makeup of these groups changes from week to week.

Confidentiality is essential for sharing, so what is said in the group stays in the group. Group members are expected to speak the truth in love (Eph 4:15). Although conversation may be frank, it must never be judgmental, nagging, abusive or cruel. Also forbidden are gossip, finger-pointing and general griping.

These questions related to accountability are suggested by Wesley's General Rules of Discipleship.

Since we last met, how have I:

- Nourished my relationship with God through acts of piety such as worship, prayer, Bible study, and discipleship?

- Shown God's grace to others through fellowship and acts of mercy such as service and witness?

- Avoided doing harm to others or myself?

- Done good to others at every opportunity as I am able?

- Endeavored to know, love, and obey God?

- Watched over others in my group in love?

If you feel it necessary, you can write a group covenant that establishes expectations for all members. Here's an example:

Answering the call of Jesus Christ to be his disciple and wishing to grow in faith and action, I make this covenant with other members of my group:

- *We will meet regularly.*

- *If I am unable to attend or may be late, I will tell someone in the group ahead of time so that my absence or lateness will not be a concern to others.*

- *I will hold the members of my group accountable for their growth in discipleship as I expect them to hold me accountable for mine.*

- *I will laugh with them, cry with them, pray for them, and encourage them.*

- *I will be sensitive to their spiritual, emotional, and physical needs.*

- *I will be open, honest, and willing to share.*

- *I will at all times speak the truth only in love.*

- *I will hold in confidence all that is shared in the group.*

- *I will never speak ill of someone who is absent or engage in any other form of gossip.*

Appendix 2

Twenty-two questions

It is said that these questions of self-examination were first used among the Oxford Methodists, starting about 1730. Sometimes spiritually on the mark, sometimes almost obsessive in their interior focus, the questions do fit Wesley's temperament at the time. You can judge whether they are of any use to you.

1. Am I consciously or unconsciously creating the impression that I am better than I really am? In other words, am I a hypocrite?

2. Am I honest in all my acts and words, or do I exaggerate?

3. Do I confidentially pass on to another what was told to me in confidence?

4. Can I be trusted?

5. Am I a slave to dress, friends, work, or habits?

6. Am I self-conscious, self-pitying, or self-justifying?

7. Did the Bible live in me today?

8. Do I give it time to speak to me every day?

9. Am I enjoying prayer?

10. When did I last speak to someone else about my faith?

11. Do I pray about the money I spend?

12. Do I get to bed on time and get up on time?

13. Do I disobey God in anything?

14. Do I insist upon doing something about which my conscience is uneasy?

15. Am I defeated in any part of my life?

16. Am I jealous, impure, critical, irritable, touchy, or distrustful?

17. How do I spend my spare time?

18. Am I proud?

19. Do I thank God that I am not as other people, especially as the Pharisees who despised the publican?

20. Is there anyone whom I fear, dislike, disown, criticize, hold a resentment toward or disregard? If so, what am I doing about it?

21. Do I grumble or complain constantly?

22. Is Christ real to me?[1]

---

1. "John Wesley's 22 Questions."

For More Reading

WESLEY'S WORKS

John Wesley's works are available in many editions, some easier to find than others. Three excellent sources on the internet are free and easy to search:

- Wesley Center Online, maintained by the Wesley Center for Applied Theology at Northwest Nazarene University in Nampa, Idaho: *http://wesley.nnu.edu.*
- Christian Classics Ethereal Library: *ccel.org*
- The Center for Studies in the Wesleyan Tradition, Duke Divinity School: http://*divinity.duke.edu/initiatives/cswt*

The longtime standard of Wesley's works was the fourteen-volume edition edited by Thomas Jackson in 1831 and reprinted in 1991 by Baker Book House of Grand Rapids from the 1872 edition by the Wesleyan Methodist Book Room, London. Sadly, it is now out of print and hard to find.

Various volumes of the scholarly Oxford/Abingdon Bicentennial Edition of Wesley's works have been published since 1960. To date, twenty-two of a projected thirty-four volumes have been published. Each volume costs $50 or more, and they are stocked by few libraries, so they are out of reach of most readers. For more information about them, see http://*wesley-works.org* and http://*Cokesbury.com.*

The best one-volume set of Wesley sermons is the one cited in the Bibliography:

Albert C. Outler & Richard P. Heitzenrater, eds., *John Wesley's Sermons*, Nashville: Abingdon, 1991.

Still available is this fine older compilation: Albert C. Outler, ed., *John Wesley*, New York: Oxford University Press, 1964.

You also can find some Wesley works at Seedbed, a publishing arm of Asbury Theological Seminary: *https://my.seedbed.com/product-category/the-john-wesley-collection/*

Besides those works listed in the Bibliography, here are some books I have found especially helpful in learning about the Wesley brothers and Wesleyan theology.

BRIEF, VERY ACCESSIBLE BOOKS ABOUT WESLEY AND THE REVIVAL

Adam Hamilton, *Revival: Faith as Wesley Lived It*. Nashville: Abingdon, 2014.
Steve Harper, *John Wesley's Message Today*. Grand Rapids: Zondervan, 1983.
Henry H. Knight III, *John Wesley: Optimist of Grace*. Eugene, OR: Cascade, 2018.
Howard A. Snyder, *The Radical Wesley*. Downers Grove, IL: InterVarsity, 1983.
Lovett H. Weems Jr., *John Wesley's Message Today*. Nashville: Abingdon, 1982, 1991.

HISTORY OF METHODISM

Paul W. Chilcote, *She Offered Them Christ: The Legacy of Women Preachers in Early Methodism*. Eugene, OR: Wipf & Stock, 2001. Reprint of Nashville: Abingdon, 1993.
Ryan N. Danker, *Constrained to Deviate: John Wesley and the Evangelical Anglicans*. *https://hdl.handle.net/2144/3756*. Boston University doctoral dissertation, 2012. (Published as *Wesley and the Anglicans: Political Divisions in Early Evangelicalism*. Downers Grove, IL: InterVarsity, 2016.)
Geordan Hammond, *John Wesley in America: Restoring Primitive Christianity*. New York: Oxford University Press, 2014.
Richard P. Heitzenrater, *Wesley & the People Called Methodists*. Nashville: Abingdon, 2013.

Donna L. Fowler-Merchant, *Mothers in Israel: Methodist Beginnings Through the Eyes of Women*. Nashville: Foundery, 2020.

Henry H. Knight III, *Anticipating Heaven Below: Optimism of Grace from Wesley to the Pentecostals*. Eugene, OR: Cascade, 2014.

Henry H. Knight III, ed., *From Aldersgate to Azusa Street: Wesleyan, Holiness and Pentecostal Visions of the New Creation*. Eugene, OR: Pickwick, 2010.

Frederick A. Norwood, *The Story of American Methodism*. Nashville: Abingdon, 1974.

Charles Yrigoyen, *John Wesley: Holiness of Heart & Life*. Nashville: Abingdon, 1999.

BIOGRAPHY

Kenneth J. Collins, *A Real Christian: The Life of John Wesley*. Nashville: Abingdon, 1999.

Richard P. Heitzenrater, *The Elusive Mr. Wesley*. Nashville: Abingdon, 2003.

Henry D. Rack, *Reasonable Enthusiast: John Wesley and the Rise of Methodism*. Nashville: Abingdon, 1995

Harry S. Stout, *The Divine Dramatist: George Whitefield and the Rise of Modern Evangelicalism*. Grand Rapids: Eerdmans, 1991.

Julian Wilson, *The Wesleys: Two Men Who Changed the World*. Franklin, TN: Authentic, 2022.

Mildred Bangs Wynkoop, *John Wesley: Christian Revolutionary*. Kansas City: Beacon Hill, 1970.

PRACTICAL APPLICATIONS

D. Michael Henderson, *John Wesley's Class Meeting: A Model for Making Disciples*. Omaheke, Namibia: Rafiki Press, 2016; reprint of Nappanee, Indiana: Francis Asbury–Evangel, 1997.

Henry H. Knight III, *Eight Life-Enriching Practices for United Methodists*. Nashville: Abingdon, 2001.

Kevin M. Watson, *A Blueprint for Discipleship: Wesley's General Rules as a Guide for Christian Living*. Nashville: Discipleship Resources, 2009.

Kevin M. Watson, *The Class Meeting: Reclaiming a Forgotten (and Essential) Small Group Experience*. Franklin, TN: Seedbed, 2014.

EXPLORING WESLEYAN THEOLOGY

Kenneth J. Collins, *The Scripture Way of Salvation: The Heart of John Wesley's Theology*. Nashville: Abingdon, 1997.

Gregory S. Clapper, *The Renewal of the Heart Is the Mission of the Church: John Wesley's Heart Religion in the Twenty-First Century*. Eugene, OR: Cascade, 2010.

Gregory S. Clapper, *As If the Heart Mattered: A Wesleyan Spirituality*. Eugene, OR: Wipf & Stock, 2014. Reprint of Nashville: Upper Room, 1997.

John B. Cobb Jr., *Grace and Responsibility: A Wesleyan Theology for Today*. Nashville: Abingdon, 1995.

H. Ray Dunning, *Grace, Faith & Holiness*. Kansas City: Beacon Hill, 1988.

H. Ray Dunning, *Reflecting the Divine Image: Christian Ethics in Wesleyan Perspective*. Downers Grove, IL: InterVarsity, 1998.

H. Ray Dunning, *Sanctification: A Layman's Guide*. Kansas City: Beacon Hill, 1991.

Henry H. Knight III, *The Presence of God in the Christian Life*. Lanham, MD: Scarecrow, 1992.

Randy L. Maddox, ed., *Aldersgate Reconsidered*. Nashville: Kingswood, 1990.

Randy L. Maddox, *Responsible Grace*. Nashville: Kingswood, 1988.

Randy L. Maddox, *Rethinking Wesley's Theology*. Nashville: Kingswood, 1998.

Thomas J. Oord and Michael Lodahl, *Relational Holiness*. Kansas City: Beacon Hill, 2005.

Albert C. Outler, *Evangelism & Theology in the Wesleyan Spirit*. Nashville: Discipleship Resources, 2003. (Combining two books individually long out of print: *Evangelism in the Wesleyan Spirit* and *Theology in the Wesleyan Spirit*.)

Mildred Bangs Wynkoop, *Foundations of Wesleyan–Arminian Theology*. Kansas City: Beacon Hill, 1967.

Bibliography

"30 Hour Famine." https://30hourfamine.worldvision.org/.

"About Us." World Methodist Council. http://worldmethodistcouncil.org/about-us.

"And Can It Be That I Should Gain." United Methodist Church, Mar 6, 2017. https://www.umc.org/en/content/and-can-it-be-that-i-should-gain-by-charles-wesley.

Belcher, Joseph. *George Whitefield: A Biography*. New York: American Tract Society, 2013.

Chambers, Oswald. *My Utmost for His Highest*. Westwood, NJ: Barbour, 1963.

Chilcote, Paul. *Recapturing the Wesleys' Vision*. Downers Grove, IL: InterVarsity, 2004.

Dozier, Verna. *The Authority of the Laity*. Washington, DC: Alban Institute, 1982.

Ferguson, Charles W. *Organizing to Beat the Devil: Methodists and the Making of America*. New York: Doubleday, 1971.

Hawn, C. Michael. "History of Hymns: 'Christ the Lord is Risen Today.'" Discipleship Ministries, Mar 31, 2021. https://www.umcdiscipleship.org/articles/history-of-hymns-christ-the-lord-is-risen-today.

———. "History of Hymns: 'Come, Let Us Use the Grace Divine.'" Discipleship Ministries, Nov 18, 2015. https://www.umcdiscipleship.org/resources/history-of-hymns-come-let-us-use-the-grace-divine.

———. "History of Hymns: 'Rejoice, the Lord is King.'" Discipleship Ministries, Oct 27, 2021. https://www.umcdiscipleship.org/articles/history-of-hymns-rejoice-the-lord-is-king.

Hehn, Jonathan. "History of Hymns: 'Jesus, Thine All-Victorious Love.'" Discipleship Ministries, Apr 27, 2016. https://www.umcdiscipleship.org/resources/history-of-hymns-jesus-thine-all-victorious-love-wesley.

"History of Hymns: 'Depth of Mercy.'" Discipleship Ministries, Sep 21, 2017. https://www.umcdiscipleship.org/resources/history-of-hymns-depth-of-mercy.

"History of Hymns: 'Love Divine, All Loves Excelling.'" Discipleship Ministries, May 20, 2013. https://www.umcdiscipleship.org/resources/history-of-hymns-love-divine-all-loves-excelling.

Holzemer, Beth R. "History of Hymns: 'Where Shall My Wondering Soul Begin.'" Discipleship Ministries, Oct 9, 2019. https://www.umcdiscipleship.org/articles/history-of-hymns-where-shall-my-wondering-soul-begin.

Job, Rueben P. *Three Simple Rules*. Nashville: Abingdon, 2007.

"John Wesley's 22 Questions of Self Examination." United Methodist Church, May 28, 2020. https://www.umc.org/en/content/john-wesleys-22-questions-of-self-examination.

"John Wesley letter to John Newton, 1765 May 14." https://digitalcollections.smu.edu/digital/collection/jwl/id/44.

Jones, Scott J. *John Wesley's Conception and Use of Scripture*. Nashville: Kingswood, 1995.

Jones, Scott J. *United Methodist Doctrine: The Extreme Center*. Nashville: Abingdon, 2002.

Kimbrough, S. T., Jr., and Kenneth G. C. Newport, eds. *The Manuscript Journal of the Reverend Charles Wesley, M.A.* Nashville: Kingswood, 2008.

Letter to John Mason: Nov 21, 1776. http://wesley.nnu.edu/john-wesley/the-letters-of-john-wesley/wesleys-letters-1776.

Letter to Miss Marsh: Mar 29, 1760. http://wesley.nnu.edu/john-wesley/the-letters-of-john-wesley/wesleys-letters-1760.

Letter to William Wilberforce: Feb 24, 1791. http://wesley.nnu.edu/john-wesley/the-letters-of-john-wesley/wesleys-letters-1791.

Lewis, Jacqui. *Fierce Love*. New York: Harmony, 2021.

Mancini, Will. "North Point Community Church Strategy Imagery." https://www.willmancini.com/north-point-community-church-strategy-imagery.

Miles, Sara. *City of God*. New York: Jericho, 2014.

Miofsky, Matt. *The Methodist Book of Daily Prayer*. Nashville: Abingdon, 2023.

Nouwen, Henri. *You Are the Beloved*. New York: Convergent, 2017.

"O For A Thousand Tongues To Sing." Discipleship Ministries, Jun 12, 2008. https://www.umcdiscipleship.org/resources/o-for-a-thousand-tongues-to-sing-18-original-stanzas.

Outler, Albert C., and Richard P. Heitzenrater, eds. *John Wesley's Sermons*. Nashville: Abingdon, 1991.

Peterson, Eugene. *A Long Obedience in the Same Direction*, Downers Grove, IL: InterVarsity, 1980.

Plantinga, Cornelius, Jr. *Not the Way It's Supposed to Be: A Breviary of Sin*. Grand Rapids: Eerdmans, 1996.

Preface to "Collection of Hymns for the Use of the People Called Methodist." https://archive.org/details/collectionofhymowesl/page/4mode/2up.

Rasmus, Rudy. *Love. Period.* Nashville: Worthy, 2014.

Runyon, Ted. *The New Creation: John Wesley's Theology Today*. Nashville: Abingdon, 1998.

United Methodist Book of Discipline. Nashville, 2016.

Walker, Robert Martin. *You Might Be a United Methodist If*. St. Louis: Chalice, 1988.

Watson, David Lowes. *Class Leaders*. Nashville: Discipleship Resources, 1991.

Wesley, Charles. May 21, 1738. http://wesley.nnu.edu/charles-wesley/the-journal-of-charles-wesley-1707-1788/the-journal-of-charles-wesley-may–1–august–31–1738.

Wesley, Charles. Journal. May 23, 1738. http://wesley.nnu.edu/charles-wesley/the-journal-of-charles-wesley-1707-1788/the-journal-of-charles-wesley-may-1-august-31-1738.

Wesley, John. *Sunday Service of the Methodists in North America*. Nashville: United Methodist Publishing, 1984.

————. "Thoughts Upon Slavery." https://docsouth.unc.edu/church/wesley/wesley.html.

Wright, N. T. *The Challenge of Easter*. Downers Grove, IL: InterVarsity, 2009.

Wynkoop, Mildred Bangs. *A Theology of Love*. Kansas City: Beacon Hill, 1972.

Printed in Great Britain
by Amazon